Theory and Practice of Teaching Medicine

Books in the ACP Teaching Medicine Series

Theory and Practice of Teaching Medicine
Jack Ende, MD, MACP
Editor

Methods for Teaching Medicine
Kelley M. Skeff, MD, PhD, MACP
Georgette A. Stratos, PhD
Editors

Teaching in Your Office, A Guide to Instructing Medical Students and Residents, Second Edition
Patrick C. Alguire, MD, FACP
Dawn E. DeWitt, MD, MSc, FACP
Linda E. Pinsky, MD, FACP
Gary S. Ferenchick, MD, FACP
Editors

Teaching in the Hospital
Jeff Wiese, MD, FACP
Editor

Mentoring in Academic Medicine
Holly J. Humphrey, MD, MACP
Editor

Leadership Careers in Medical Education
Louis Pangaro, MD, MACP
Editor

Teaching Medicine Series

Jack Ende, MD, MACP
Series Editor

Theory and Practice of Teaching Medicine

Jack Ende, MD, MACP
Editor

ACP Press
American College of Physicians • Philadelphia, Pennsylvania

Director, Publishing Operations: Linda Drumheller
Developmental Editor: Marla Sussman
Production Editor: Suzanne Meyers
Publishing Coordinator: Angela Gabella
Cover Design: Kate Nichols
Index: Kathleen Patterson

Printed in the United States of America
Printing/Binding by Versa Press
Composition by ACP Graphic Services

Library of Congress Cataloging-in-Publication Data

Theory and practice of teaching medicine / [edited by] Jack Ende.
    p. ; cm. -- (ACP teaching medicine series)
  Includes bibliographical references and index.
  ISBN 978-1-934465-41-7
  1. Medicine--Study and teaching. I. Ende, Jack. II. American College of
Physicians. III. Series: ACP teaching medicine series.
  [DNLM: 1. Education, Medical. 2. Teaching--methods. W 18 T396 2010]
  R735.T54 2010
  610.76--dc22
                              2009053101

10 11 12 13 14 / 10 9 8 7 6 5 4 3 2 1

Contributors

Judith L. Bowen, MD, FACP
Professor of Medicine
Oregon Health & Science University
Portland, Oregon

Jack Ende, MD, MACP
Professor of Medicine
University of Pennsylvania School
    of Medicine
Chief, Department of Medicine
Penn Presbyterian Medical Center
Philadelphia, Pennsylvania

B. Graeme Fincke, MD
Associate Professor
Boston University School of Medicine
Boston, Massachusetts

William Hersh, MD, FACP
Professor and Chair
Department of Medical Informatics and
    Clinical Epidemiology
Oregon Health and Science University
Portland, Oregon

Jay D. Orlander, MD, MPH
Professor of Medicine
Evans Department of Medicine
Boston University School of Medicine
Associate Chief, Medical Service
Veterans Affairs Boston Healthcare
    System
Boston, Massachusetts

C. Scott Smith, MD, FACP
Professor of General Internal Medicine
Adjunct Professor
Medical Education and Biomedical
    Informatics
University of Washington
Veterans Affairs Medical Center
Boise, Idaho

Yvonne Steinert, PhD
Director, Centre for Medical Education
Associate Dean, Faculty Development
Faculty of Medicine
McGill University
Montreal, Quebec, Canada

*To my teachers, colleagues, and patients, who allowed me to learn,
and to my students, residents, and their patients, who allowed me to teach.
This book and series are dedicated to them.*

Acknowledgments

So many individuals contributed to this book series. Patrick Alguire and Steve Weinberger deserve special recognition for having first conceived of the idea of developing a curriculum—and then a book series—that lays out what medical teachers and educators need to know, or at least consider. Robert Spanier and his staff, particularly Angela Gabella, helped move this grand scheme into a six-part reality. Marla Sussman provided outstanding editorial direction, and Suzanne Meyers helped to develop the final copy. Catherine Greco provided outstanding administrative assistance throughout this entire process. The authors authored, the editors edited (and authored), and in the end we all hope we have helped medical teachers understand more about what they—and we—do.

Contents

Visit www.acponline.org/acp_press/teaching
for additional information.

About the *Teaching Medicine* Series

This book series, *Teaching Medicine*, represents a major initiative from the American College of Physicians. It is intended for College members but also for the profession as a whole. Internists, family physicians, subspecialists, surgical colleagues, nurse practitioners, and physician assistants—indeed, anyone involved with medical education—should find this book series useful as they pursue one of the greatest privileges of the profession: the opportunity to teach and make a difference in the lives of learners and their patients. The series is composed of six books:

- *Theory and Practice of Teaching Medicine*, edited by me, considers how medical learners learn (how to be doctors), how medical teachers teach, and how they (the teachers) might learn to teach better.

- *Methods for Teaching Medicine*, edited by Kelley M. Skeff and Georgette A. Stratos, builds on this foundation but focuses on the actual methods that medical teachers use. This book explores the full range of techniques that encourage learning within groups. The authors present a conceptual framework and guiding perspectives for understanding teaching; the factors that support choices for particular teaching methods (such as lecturing vs. small group discussion); and practical advice for preceptors, attendings, lecturers, discussion leaders, workshop leaders, and, finally, course directors charged with running programs for continuing medical education.

- *Teaching in Your Office,* edited by Patrick C. Alguire, Dawn E. DeWitt, Linda E. Pinsky, and Gary S. Ferenchick, will be familiar to many teaching internists. It has been reissued as part of this series. This book remains the office-based preceptor's single most useful resource for preparing to receive medical students and residents into an ambulatory practice setting or, among those already engaged in office-based teaching, for learning how to do it even better.

- *Teaching in the Hospital* is edited by Jeff Wiese and considers the challenges and rewards of teaching in that particular setting. Hospitalists as well as more traditional internists who attend on the inpatient service will be interested in the insightful advice that this book provides. This advice focuses not only on how to conduct rounds and encourage learning among students and house officers but also on how to frame and orient the content of rounds for some of the more frequently encountered inpatient conditions.

- *Mentoring in Academic Medicine,* edited by Holly J. Humphrey, considers professional development across the continuum of medical education, from issues pertaining to students to residents to faculty themselves, as well as issues pertaining to professional development of special populations. Here is where the important contributions of mentors and role models are explored in detail.

- *Leadership Careers in Medical Education* concludes this series. Edited by Louis Pangaro, this book is written for members of the medical faculty who are pursuing—or who are considering—careers as clerkship directors, residency program directors, or educational leaders of departments or medical schools, careers that require not only leadership skill but also a deep understanding of the organization and administration of internal medicine's educational enterprise. This book explores the theory and practice of educational leadership, including curricular design and evaluation; and offers insightful profiles of many of internal medicine's most prominent leaders.

Jack Ende, MD, MACP
Philadelphia, 2010

Introduction: Facing the Challenges of Medical Teaching

There used to be a sign in the photo shop where I had slides made (back when slides were actually made rather than saved on a computer). The sign read, "We can make it fast. We can make it cheap. We can make it good. Pick two."

Welcome to the rewarding but challenging world of medical education, where faculty must be concerned with meeting the needs of the learner, providing effective care for the patient, and doing this all in an appropriate amount of time. And welcome as well to the American College of Physicians' faculty development book series, *Teaching Medicine*; the first book, *Theory and Practice of Teaching Medicine*; and some of the more intriguing challenges faced by medical educators.

The term *challenges*, as distinct from *decisions*, is chosen deliberately. While K through 12 classroom teaching has been framed in the education literature as a series of decisions (1), some explicit and others implicit, medical teaching is better examined through a wider lens. Medical teachers make decisions that affect their teaching all the time (and often without time). Decision-making, however, implies choosing among alternatives and hardly captures the complexity and nuances of medical education. Medical teaching is not that simple.

Rather, medical teaching, both formal and informal, preclinical and clinical, planned and impromptu, is complex, and is better considered as a series of challenges. These challenges certainly can be avoided, as can teaching itself. Indeed, it is not unheard of for physicians, including medical school faculty, to choose to "opt out" of teaching and to pursue careers focused on clinical care, or research, or administration. Moreover, of physicians who do choose to make teaching a significant part of their careers, few teach full-time; fewer still are paid to teach. While we have come a long way from the days of voluntary faculty (2), it is important to appreciate that, for the most part, physicians who do teach have "signed-on"; they have agreed to face the challenges inherent in teaching.

This book, and this book series, is written for them: the physicians who choose to teach. They are the custodians of medical knowledge, the caretakers of the profession, and the midwives of the next generation of physicians. They are the members of the medical community who, for any number of reasons, look forward to meeting the challenges of working with students, residents, fellows, and faculty, enabling them, their learners, to become better equipped to care for their patients, more thoughtful as professionals, and more personally fulfilled. Medical teachers know how exhilarating that can be.

They also know how frustrating or confusing medical teaching can be. That is why it is so important that medical teachers take the time to reflect and consider the challenges they will encounter. This introduction presents some of the more fundamental challenges of teaching medicine, particularly those that have intrigued me during my 30 or so years of trying to get it right. It begins with the challenge of determining what to teach, both formally and informally, and considers as well the challenges of making teaching more purposeful, complementary to patient care, and more fun. It also addresses challenges related to encouraging professionalism, developing moral character, and affecting the tone and climate of medical teaching. Finally, it explores the challenge of how medical teaching can be made more rewarding for teachers. This final challenge is critically important and is not discussed often enough. This introduction ends with an overview of the other chapters in this book, where more fully developed discussions of the challenges raised here are likely to be found.

❖ How Do You Decide What to Teach?

Suppose you are asked to organize an elective in women's health. You most likely would consider what to include according to the questions one poses when developing a curriculum. Discussed more fully in another book in this series, *Leadership Careers in Medical Education*, these questions might be, What do my learners already know? What do they need to know? What should they be able to do? What forms of instruction are available? How might all this best be organized? How can I measure my success? A similar process would define the considerations you would entertain before planning a lecture (discussed in the book *Methods for Teaching Medicine*). But what about less formal teaching, such as precepting in the office, when a student presents a patient with asthma, or attending in the hospital, when an intern presents a patient with congestive heart failure? Although office-based and hospital-based teaching are often improvisational, they should not be random, nor determined exclusively by the interests of the teacher or what he or she knows best. Rather, the goals of the teaching should be to assure that the patient is well cared for, of course, but also to meet the learning needs of the students. The more you know about your students, what they already know, and what they need to learn, the more effective your teaching will be. And so we typically follow the students' case presentation with a question: "What do you think is going on?" And then we listen—carefully—to determine what the student knows, how she thinks. Only then can we begin to effectively teach. Christenson and colleagues (3) said it best, "Our knowledge of students helps us meet them 'where they are.' And that is where learning begins." And never forget that when it comes to office-based and hospital-based teaching, generally less is more.

❖ How Can Teaching That Is Impromptu Also Be Purposeful?

Anyone familiar with white-water rafting knows what it is like to conduct rounds in a busy inpatient unit, no less an emergency department or intensive care unit. A crowded office is not much less turbulent. Add to that the pressure of time, less-than-well-organized case presentations, and the imperative that regardless of rounds, patients need to receive proper care, and the stage is set for a wild ride indeed. How can clinical teachers find a sense of organization, or at least a rudder, to keep things moving in the right direction? How can impromptu teaching also be purposeful?

Two recommendations are worth considering. First, as described in the third book, *Teaching in Your Office*, and elsewhere, several frameworks are designed specifically for this purpose. The five-step micro-skills model (4), the SNAPPS model (5), and other models (6) enable clinical teachers to impose just the right amount of structure to assure that teaching is purposeful. Second, develop a repertoire of teaching scripts as described in *Methods for Teaching Medicine* and *Teaching in the Hospital* and elsewhere (7). Shulman (8) would have called these scripts "pedagogic content knowledge," his term for an organized approach to a teaching topic, often including algorithms, demonstrations, diagrams, and mini-lectures, conveying useful representations of key concepts, which enable teachers to guide learners along an educationally fruitful path. Common diseases are common. Be prepared to teach about diseases or clinical problems that are most likely to be encountered. And modify scripts to ensure that they are up to date and meet the learners' needs.

Third, develop what Brookfield (9) has called an *organizing vision* for teaching—a series of beliefs and values about teaching that reflect what you consider most important for patient care, learners' needs, and that fit with your particular strengths. For some, that may be physical diagnosis; for others, evidence-based medicine. Without being too idiosyncratic or ideological, be certain your teaching is authentic and expresses what you believe to be most important. Students will sense that.

❖ How Can Teaching Complement Patient Care?

Clinical medical education, based as it is in real clinical settings, is envied by other professions. Law schools have had to create moot courts; architecture schools, ateliers. Medical schools just open the hospital doors. Ludmerer (10) reminds us that this has not always been the case; in fact, gaining access to clinical settings is one of the most important and hard-fought achievements of the early-20th-century medical educators. What a pity it would be if clinical teachers failed to take full advantage.

Pedagogy should not take center stage in clinical teaching. That position belongs to clinical skill. Clinical expertise and the ratings that faculty achieve on their teaching evaluations overlap greatly, and that's as it should be. Again Shulman (8) wrote about the intersection of pedagogic knowledge and content knowledge. Both are needed for effective teaching. Faculty who understand the principles of teaching but lack clinical knowledge and skill are as ineffective as faculty who are skilled at caring for patients but not in relating to learners. Medical expertise and teaching expertise harmonize most beautifully when the skilled practitioner and learner collaborate to solve real problems, particularly the tough ones. Often times this entails the teacher making explicit, or overt, what otherwise would be implicit, or covert. Schön (11) calls this reflection-in-action. He describes moments when "the coaches' and learners' dialogues flow gracefully, almost effortlessly, their attention focused on the problem at hand. They seem absorbed. They speak in half sentences, often completing each others' thoughts. Time passes quickly; the energy level is high" (12). While the basic tenet of experiential learning is that the learner "goes first" and encounters the clinical problem before the teacher, we should never underestimate the power of thinking out loud, inviting our learners to be collaborators, and solving problems together with them.

❖ How Can You Judge Your Learners' Readiness to Assume Responsibility?

Providing students, residents, and fellows with incremental responsibility is a cornerstone of medical education, particularly at the graduate level. Several models have been developed to assess and categorize learners' readiness to assume responsibility; Pangaro's four-stage RIME model is the most accepted, particularly for students (RIME refers to a trainee's progression from "reporter" to "interpreter" to "manager" and "educator") (13). For residents and fellows, however, the determination that competency has been attained and readiness for responsibility has been achieved is another matter. Attending-level supervision is mandatory; that goes without saying. But within that overarching tenet there remains a great deal of leeway. Some residents and fellows can be entrusted with substantial responsibility; others require more careful supervision. Attendings must be sensitive and careful observers, able to perceive when trainees are ready to manage clinical decisions or perform procedures, and when they need more careful supervision. Self-assessment may not be reliable. Research findings (14) sound a cautionary note. Data suggest a poor correlation between self-assessment and competency, with most trainees tending to overestimate their ability. The worst offenders are those in the lowest quartiles of performance. Other work suggests that trainees are reluctant to ask for help (15). While this may not pertain to *our* residents (or ourselves), the data do underscore the importance of objective tests of competency, more sophisticated systems of evaluation, and, again, careful supervision and skilled mentorship. It is not easy to provide trainees with accurate assessment while maintaining their self-confidence and your relationship with them.

❖ When Should You Criticize Rather Than Allow Things to Pass?

Data suggest that medical teachers often fail to criticize when inappropriate behaviors are observed (16). The reasons for this, of course, are several, including a desire to maintain the relationship with the learner or to protect his or her self-esteem, or simply an inappropriate threshold for determining that standards have been abridged. Clinical faculty are the custodians of professionalism. If *they* do not maintain high standards, even zero tolerance for lapses in professionalism, then the status of physicians as professionals, in all senses of the word, is at risk.

What sort of behaviors warrant criticism? Any that are at odds with the standards of the profession (17) and negatively affect patients, the care team, or systems of care. Weisinger (18) urges us to "befriend criticism" and use it as a tool to improve individual and organizational success. Be certain of your criteria for criticizing, identify those criteria to your learner, and rely on the techniques of effective feedback to alert learners to first, what they have done; second, the real or potential consequences of their actions; and third, and most important, how they can do better in the future. Particularly in areas related to professional behavior, we all need to carefully observe, criticize, and observe again what our learners do.

❖ Can We Affect Moral Character?

This question lies at the heart of all our attempts to improve our learners' skills in areas of humanism and professionalism. For the latter, Huddle's (19) comments are particularly germane: "As attractive as it may be to view professionalism as expertise or as a competency, I would contend that in asking for professionalism, that is, for just, altruistic, conscientious, and compassionate physicians and trainees, medical educators are asking for morality, which is at the bottom asking for more than expertise." He continues,

> Professionalism and training means taking the time and making the effort to do the right thing when the path of least resistance would be to take an easier way out, allowing the demands of, say, the next half-hour, or one's hunger or anxiety or fatigue or desire to leave the hospital, to override moral considerations. In asking for professionalism, medical educators are asking for compassion, kindness, honesty, and intellectual rigor all to be exercised when the chips are down. … That is not to say that professionalism can-

not be inculcated during medical training. But I suggest that the task may be harder than we think and may require of medical educators a degree of personal virtue and involvement with trainees that most of us perhaps do not really contemplate, let alone achieve."

Without minimizing the importance of lectures, seminars, rounds, and workshops designed to encourage professionalism and humanistic behavior, faculty should never underestimate their own importance as mentors and role models, nor the importance of the time they spend being close to, and working with, students, residents, and fellows.

❖ What Can Teachers Do to Ensure That Rounds Are Viewed as Important?

Much of the teaching carried out in medical settings is "mandatory." No one is allowed to *miss* rounds. Yet the degree of enthusiasm learners display toward clinical teaching activities varies greatly. Just observe. Is the team gathering on time? Is everyone paying attention? Are people really listening and doing their utmost to hold distractions at bay? While a good deal of this variation is attributable to factors pertaining to the teacher and to the learners themselves, there also is a good deal that is attributable to the context.

Subtitled *How Little Things Can Make a Big Difference*, Malcolm Gladwell's book *The Tipping Point* (20) describes how behaviors are a function of environment. Personal and social factors count, of course. But so too, often in strikingly powerful ways, do external factors, such as the physical setting. Gladwell describes the "broken windows" theory, in which crime is considered a result of disorder, even a result of the ambiance. "If a window is broken and left unrepaired," he writes, "people walking by will conclude that no one cares and no one is in charge. Soon, more windows will be broken," or worse. Another example of what Gladwell refers to as the "power of context" is found in an interesting experiment carried out at the Princeton Theological Seminary, which demonstrated that even very recent study of the biblical story of the Good Samaritan—by seminarians, no less—had little or no impact on the seminarian's decision to stop or not stop and assist a man in distress encountered on the street. What did matter was whether the seminarians believed they were late for an upcoming exam versus whether they had a few minutes to spare.

What does the "power of context" have to do with medical education? Actually, a great deal. If students observe that faculty show up late for a lecture, they will as well. If teaching rooms used for rounds are messy, so too will be the students' presentations. If residents are not given enough time to spend with their patients, even residents with the best of intentions will begin to cut corners. The point is that the environment, indeed all the contextual factors that come into play in medical education, should be scrutinized by the faculty and receive proper attention. Old paper coffee cups on the table may not lead to bad patient care, but they certainly are not helping rounds.

❖ How Can Clinical Teaching Be Made More Interesting, Even Fun?

Another way to view the context within which clinical medical education takes place is to note the climate. Skeff and Stratos (in another book in the series, *Methods for Teaching Medicine*) describe a powerful seven-category framework for analyzing teaching; category 1 is the learning climate. Defined by Skeff and Stratos as "the tone or atmosphere of the teaching setting, including whether it is stimulating and whether learners can comfortably identify and address their limitations," learning climate essentially answers the question, "Do the learners want to be there?"

Medical educators are fortunate in that they teach about real cases. At its best, clinical teaching helps learners solve problems that they hope to solve. But fatigue, distractions, and stress always are in the background in medical education, and faculty should do as much as possible to keep things interesting and even fun. Stories, jokes, games, and contests all can be incorporated into medical teaching. Anything that encourages a more upbeat learning climate is worth considering.

An equally important question may be, "Does the teacher want to be there?" Medical teaching is hard. Everyone knows that. The trials and tribulations of medical teaching are never far from view. Less clear, however, are the sources of joy that come with teaching. And there is no substitute for the teachers' enthusiasm.

❖ How Can Teachers "Preserve the Passion"?

Communicating about teaching in general, Brookfield (21) a nonmedical educator, writes, "Passion, hope, doubt, fear, exhilaration, weariness, colleagueship, loneliness, glorious defeats, hollow victories, and, above all, the certainties of surprise and ambiguity—how on earth can a single word or phrase begin to capture the multilayer complexity of what it feels like to teach?" Add to that the complexities and pressures of practicing medicine simultaneously with teaching and you begin to understand why it is so critical that teachers take steps to preserve the passion (22). It may not renew on its own.

Several lessons can be learned from the field of emotional intelligence (23), particularly how to set achievable goals, manage time, control emotions, and celebrate victories. Other recommendations are more specific to medical educators. First, find a colleague, perhaps a mentor, someone who teaches in a format similar to yours and talk about your (and his or her) teaching. Whether these conversations are used for seeking advice, sharing successes, or just keeping in touch, having someone to talk to about teaching can help a great deal.

Second, develop your own barometer for how well you are doing as a teacher. Learner evaluations are helpful, and certainly teaching awards are as well, but they may not tell the whole, or the real, story. Decide what your goals are and determine for yourself how you will know if you have succeeded. In chapter 4 of this book, Steinert provides a more detailed approach to doing just that.

Third, keep track of your students, and encourage them to stay in touch with you. Like a physician hearing years later from a grateful patient, a medical teacher can derive enormous satisfaction from the contact he or she maintains with past students.

Fourth, read about the history of medical education. Appreciate that as a medical teacher you are part of a tradition that has included all the Oslerian giants of years past and that you are taking your place today alongside the best that our profession has to offer. And read about medical education theory and research. The more one appreciates the contingencies, options, and strategies that support each decision that is made—or not made—the more one marvels at the process of teaching and learning.

Fifth, engage in faculty development. This enriches our understanding of the process of medical education, while refreshing teaching techniques and even providing some new things to try.

Sixth, use teaching as a stimulus to maintain and enrich one's medical knowledge. There is great satisfaction in mastering a subject, and few more compelling reasons to do so than having to teach it.

And seventh, as Orlander and Fincke reminds us in chapter 3 of this book, learn as much as possible about your learners. They will come from diverse backgrounds; all will bring to their tasks a lifetime of experiences. Whether they are as young as your own children, or just a few years younger than yourself, remember that for them—and for their patients—you have an enormous opportunity to make a difference.

❖ About This Book

Theory and Practice of Teaching Medicine is intended, therefore, to lay the foundation for the others in the series. It includes this introduction, in which I consider some of the questions that have been important to me throughout my many years as a medical teacher; I hope these questions will be of interest to you, the reader. I am more certain that you will be able to improve upon the answers that I have provided, particularly after reading the chapters offered by my colleagues. In chapters 1 and 2, Judith Bowen and C. Scott Smith consider the educational theories that explain how students and residents learn and how we, as teachers, can assess where a given learner is on his or her path toward developing expertise. Chapter 1 presents the dominant explanatory theories, and chapter 2 provides examples of how those theories can be applied in actual teaching practice. In chapter 3, Jay Orlander and Graeme Fincke distill the behaviors of the most effective teachers, and in chapter 4, Yvonne Steinert considers how teachers can become better, by reflecting on the teaching they have done and accessing the most effective programs in faculty development. In chapter 5, William Hirsh provides a guide for how teachers can maintain and enrich their funds of knowledge and become more sophisticated consumers of all that computer-based systems can provide. The book concludes with a series of true stories, "Memorable Moments in Teaching and Learning," provided by members of the American College of Physicians. These stories recount the contributors' most vivid memories as teachers or learners, and gave me opportunities to consider their recollections in the light of the concepts developed by the authors of the chapters in this book and the other books in the series.

Jack Ende, MD, MACP
Philadelphia, Pennsylvania, 2010

REFERENCES

1. **Sparks-Langer GM, Starks AJ, Pasch M, Burke W, Moody CD, Gardner TG.** Teaching as Decision Making: Successful Practices for the Secondary Teacher. Upper Saddle River, NJ: Prentice Hall; 2003.

2. **Ludmerer KM.** Time to Heal: American Medical Education from the Turn of the Century to the Era of Managed Care. New York: Oxford Univ Pr; 1999.

3. **Christensen CR, Garvin DA, Sweet A.** Education for Judgment: The Artistry of Discussion Leadership. Boston: Harvard Business School Pr; 1991:26.

4. **Neher JO, Gordon KC, Meyer B, Stevens N.** A five-step "microskills" model of clinical teaching. J Am Board Fam Pract. 1992;5:419-24.

5. **Wolpaw TM, Wolpaw DR, Papp KK.** SNAPPS: a learner-centered model for outpatient education. Acad Med. 2003;78:893-8.

6. **Alguire PC, DeWitt DE, Pinsky LE, Ferenchick GS.** Teaching in Your Office: A Guide to Instructing Medical Students and Residents. 2nd ed. Philadelphia: ACP Pr; 2008:51-73.

7. **Irby DM.** What clinical teachers in medicine need to know. Acad Med. 1994;69:333-42.

8. **Shulman LS.** Knowledge and teaching: foundations of the new reform. Harvard Educational Review. 1987;57:1-22.

9. **Brookfield SD.** The Skillful Teacher. San Francisco, CA: Jossey-Bass; 1990:253-79.

10. **Ludmerer KM.** Learning to Heal: The Development of American Medical Education. New York: Basic Books; 1985.

11. **Schön DA.** The Reflective Practitioner: How Professionals Think in Action. New York: Basic Books; 1983.

12. **Ende J.** Reflections on teaching: an essay based on two books by Donald A. Schon. J Gen Intern Med. 1990;5:183-5.

13. **Pangaro L.** A new vocabulary and other innovations for improving descriptive in-training evaluations. Acad Med. 1999;74:1203-7.

14. **Ward M, Gruppen L, Regehr G.** Measuring self-assessment: current state of the art. Adv Health Sci Educ Theory Pract. 2002;7:63-80.

15. **Kennedy TJ, Regehr G, Baker GR, Lingard LA.** 'It's a cultural expectation...' The pressure on medical trainees to work independently in clinical practice. Med Educ. 2009; 43:645-53.

16. **Ginsburg S, Lingard L, Regehr G, Underwood K.** Know when to rock the boat: how faculty rationalize students' behaviors. J Gen Intern Med. 2008;23:942-7.

17. **ABIM Foundation, ACP–ASIM Foundation, and European Federation of Internal Medicine.** Medical professionalism in the new millennium: a physician charter. Ann Intern Med. 2002;136:243-6.

18. **Weisinger H.** The Power of Positive Criticism. New York: AMACOM; 1999.

19. **Huddle TS.** Teaching professionalism: is medical morality a competency? Acad Med. 2005;80:885-91.

20. **Gladwell M.** The Tipping Point: How Little Things Can Make a Big Difference. Boston: Little, Brown; 2000.

21. **Brookfield SD.** The Skillful Teacher. San Francisco, CA: Jossey-Bass; 1990:1.

22. **Manning PR, DeBakey L.** Medicine: Preserving the Passion. New York: Springer-Verlag; 1987.

23. **Weisinger H.** Emotional Intelligence at Work. San Francisco, CA: Jossey-Bass; 1998.

1

The Journey From Novice to Professional: How Theories of Learning Can Enhance Teaching

Judith L. Bowen, MD, FACP
C. Scott Smith, MD, FACP

U nderstanding how doctors learn and are influenced by their learning environments can help teachers facilitate learning. This chapter describes four theories of learning that have implications for medical education; the chapter that follows considers application of these theories to common learning problems. Behavioral theory, the oldest and probably most familiar, provides a model for learning skills and evaluating behaviors. Cognitive learning theory provides the foundation for understanding how knowledge is built, stored, and retrieved for use in clinical reasoning. Social learning theory provides a model for understanding attitudes and shared influences in the learning environment. Because most clinical education occurs in the clinical environment, with medical students and residents caring for patients, we close this chapter with a description of experiential learning theory and its relationship to the other three foundational theories.

❖ Behavioral Learning Theory

Premise
Learning is manifested by a change in observable action, which is influenced in predictable ways by external factors.

KEY POINTS

- Learning theory can provide a structure for teaching, especially when the teacher detects a learner difficulty.
- A behavioral approach is useful when dealing with a skill that can be completely evaluated with a measurable action.
- A cognitive approach is useful when dealing with clinical reasoning, and the best starting point is asking the learner to identify the type of clinical problem the learner is facing.
- A social approach is useful when dealing with attitudes and group dynamics, and should be based on shared core values.
- An experiential approach calls for reflection, and should include adequate time and continuity between learner and teacher.

Overview

Early work in classical and operant conditioning helped to make behaviorism the dominant paradigm in psychology and learning (especially in the United States) for the first half of the 20th century. The objectivity presumed in this approach continues to influence medical education today in areas such as curriculum design, testing, and competencies.

Background

In the early 1900s, work by Pavlov on classical conditioning (association between two stimuli, such as a bell tone and food) and by Watson, Skinner, and others on operant conditioning (association between a behavior and its consequences) created norms for psychology and learning theory that influenced the next several decades. The appeal of a method that was "scientific," relying only on observations without the need to resort to ill-defined hypothetical intermediate states such as "concepts" was, and remains, persuasive. The focus then in education became which rewards, punishments, and manipulated expectations could influence observable behavior in the desired direction.

Behaviorism has strongly influenced medical education. For example, curriculum is often conceptualized by using some version of the ADDIE model (analysis, design, development, implementation, evaluation) (1). This approach assumes that instruction can be designed to achieve goal-based end points by manipulating educational experiences and sequencing.

Evaluation techniques are now frequently behaviorally based. A "standardized patient" is an individual trained to portray a real patient and objectively evaluate the student with a checklist (2). Harden and colleagues (3) expanded this to the multistation behavioral evaluation known as an objective structured clinical examination (OSCE). Given enough stations, OSCEs have psychometric properties sufficient for high-stakes evaluation of physical examination skills, diagnostic acumen, and patient–physician communication.

Finally, medical education over the past 2 decades has seen a worldwide change in focus from the *process* of training (which things are taught and how) to the *outcomes* of training (competency—what is actually learned). The behavioral viewpoint is reflected in competency-based outcome initiatives from the United States (4, 5), the United Kingdom (6), and Canada (7).

Application

Behavioral theories provide the foundation for performance-based education and evaluation. It is important to establish a framework in advance for dealing with learner difficulties, such as creating explicit lists of essential job performance requirements, identifying critical support resources (mental health professionals, state-specific impaired physician programs, disability evaluators), and orienting learners and faculty to expectations and resources. Classifying the difficulty is important because the approach to each may vary (for example, mentored close supervision, due legal process, accommodating disabilities). Table 1-1 shows a useful framework for approaching the learner who is not meeting a performance goal. Goals related to professionalism and other "high-order" behavior may also require behavioral approaches.

Examples of Teaching Methods Grounded in Behavioral Learning Theory

Mastery Learning

Instead of setting aside a fixed time for a skill-based learning activity (such as advanced cardiac life support), one can define a stringent cut-point on a checklist of behaviors that constitute mastery of the topic. Students are then provided the opportunity to practice the behavior on simulators with performance feedback until they achieve mastery. On average, most of the learners will achieve mastery in the timeframe previously allotted to the class (8). However, with just a few more minutes most learners will achieve mastery. The advantages include an increased number of learners meeting mastery level. However, this approach requires variable time in the curriculum for each learner and multiple versions of the "test" (to provide enough practice with feedback); both may be significant obstacles.

Table 1-1. Behavioral Framework for Approaching Learners With Unmet Performance Goals

Category	Examples of Unmet Performance Goals	Program Needs to Establish:	Faculty Needs to:	Common Stumbling Blocks
Cognitive	Inadequate knowledge base Memory difficulties Poor reading skills	Graduated learning objectives	Gather and interpret faculty academic judgment	Moving from helping to remediation
Professionalism	Poor teamwork Chronic tardiness Inaccurate record keeping	Explicit benchmarks for professionalism	Gather and interpret evaluations from staff and peers	Lack of data
Performance	Learning disability Substance abuse Medical/psychiatric disorder	Available critical support resources (mental health professionals, state-specific impaired physician programs, disability evaluators)	Keep in mind the Rehabilitation Act and the Americans with Disabilities Act List essential job functions	Misunderstanding of process and requirements Confidentiality requirements

Data obtained from Smith CS, Stevens NG, Servis M. A general framework for approaching the resident in difficulty. Fam Med. 2007;39:331-6.

Objective Structured Clinical Examinations
OSCEs are a popular way to test many clinical competencies. They may be created by defining a target area for testing (such as chest pain). Then important tasks within that problem are identified (take a history, interpret an electrocardiogram, perform adequate cardiopulmonary resuscitation). Finally, a set of stations is designed, each of which tests some of those tasks. Actors may be trained for some stations, for instance to portray an emergency department patient with chest pain and assess history-taking and physical examination skills with checklists. Others may be simulator-, radiography-, or electrocardiography-based. Multistation 90-minute OSCEs combined with a free-response-item written test can achieve reliability sufficient for high-stakes examinations (9). Box 1-1 summarizes implications for teachers that follow from behavioral learning theory.

❖ Cognitive Learning Theory

Premise
Cognitive learning theory assumes that memory structures and abstract problem representation are critical elements of clinical reasoning. This

---

Box 1-1. Behavioral Learning Theory: Implications for Teachers

- ▶ Behavioral learning theory is best used when trying to teach skills.
- ▶ The behavioral approach should be used when the skill can be completely evaluated by using objective measurable behaviors.
- ▶ Although behavioral approaches seem rigorously objective, there is often a significant amount of interobserver variation in behavioral evaluation systems. Learners may have positive or negative "halo" effects based on clinical teachers' experiences with the same learner over time, or by reputation.
- ▶ When behavioral approaches are used for formative feedback, multiple observations and data points are required.
- ▶ Behavioral checklists may be inadequate for some competencies, such as professionalism, diagnostic reasoning, and other aspects of patient care.

theory examines how doctors convert the patient's story of illness and contextual factors into diagnoses and strategies for testing and treatment.

Overview

When faced with the task of addressing a patient's chief concern for seeking medical care, the physician must gather information, make sense of it, generate plausible explanations, and negotiate a course of action. Many times, physicians must take action in the face of uncertainty and ambiguity. Expert physicians bring to bear extensive knowledge, flexibility in reasoning strategies, monitoring strategies to reduce errors and biases, and motivation for lifelong learning. How does the educational process influence beginning medical students, who are strangers to these tasks, and develop them into proficient diagnosticians ready for independent practice? Medical education research provides some guidance.

Over the past 3 decades, research on the diagnostic reasoning processes of physicians has advanced our understanding of the way knowledge is stored in memory, retrieved for use in clinical reasoning, and applied as reasoning strategies, including heuristics. Early research attempted to identify general reasoning strategies that experts used in solving clinical problems. Instead, researchers discovered that expertise was specific to the domain of the expert (10). For example, a nephrologist deftly able to solve complex problems related to kidney disease performed no better than beginners on clinical cases in areas of medicine unrelated to nephrology.

Cognitive researchers then turned to the study of differences between beginning (novices) and experienced (experts) clinicians to better elucidate the clinical reasoning process. Two pathways toward clinical reasoning were identified. The dominant pathway taken by less experienced clinicians and clinicians facing ill-defined, ambiguous clinical problems uses "analytic" or "reflective" reasoning. The pathway taken by more experienced clinicians facing problems familiar to them uses "nonanalytic" or "automatic" reasoning, and is often described as "pattern recognition" (11). New evidence suggests that a combined reasoning strategy may be superior for reaching the correct diagnosis for all but the most basic, familiar, straightforward clinical cases (12).

Background

Sufficient medical knowledge is fundamental for successful diagnostic reasoning, although extensive knowledge does not assure success in coming to the correct diagnosis. Considerable research has explored the relationship between how knowledge may be stored in memory and efficient recall of relevant knowledge for use in reasoning through a clinical problem.

Memory Structures

The human brain's capacity for holding information in short-term (working) memory is poor. Research suggests one can consider a maximum of 7 to 10 individual pieces of information in short-term memory at one time. Thus, the more information is "chunked" into concepts, the more information (as chunks) is available for mental manipulation during reasoning. In addition, the speed with which relevant information is retrieved is related to the strength of neuronal connection between the trigger and the necessary knowledge. Building such connections is critical for knowledge and application.

For clinical medical education, the patient's presentation is the trigger for activating relevant knowledge. As clinical exposure and experience accumulate, the symptoms and signs associated with a diagnosis are "chunked" together in memory as a *syndrome* and stored in memory in categories organized around prototypical cases for the category. For example, a typical case of community-acquired pneumococcal pneumonia would serve as the anchor prototype for other cases of pneumonia.

One theory postulates that this knowledge is stored as an "illness script." These scripts have three parts: predisposing factors, pathophysiologic insult, and consequences (the clinical presentation) (13, 14). The patient's story triggers mental searching for relevant illness scripts, selection of a script, and subsequent verification of the illness script. For example, a patient presenting with fever and cough will probably trigger a *search* for illness scripts stored in memory that include the key features in the clinical presentation. During early information gathering, the syndrome of general malaise, fever, shaking chills, cough productive of purulent sputum, and difficulty breathing will probably trigger *selection* of the physician's illness script for pneumonia. Seeking to *verify* this illness script, the physician then looks for information to "fill in" the predisposing factors, asking the patient about his health status, exposures, immunizations, and so on. For complex, ill-defined clinical presentations, multiple illness scripts may be considered simultaneously, with the script verification process determining which illness scripts are retained and which are discarded in the process of generating plausible diagnostic hypotheses. With experience, the illness scripts are expanded to account for the range of presentations of the conditions, both typical and atypical.

Another theory suggests that physicians store actual clinical cases in memory, called "exemplars" or "instance scripts" (15). Often these cases are memorable experiences, associated with an emotionally charged experience in caring for a patient and learning about the patient's illness. These emotions can be intensely positive or negative. When such memories are triggered, the physician can often recall precise details about the patient, the circumstances, and other contextual factors. For example, assisting in the care of one's first patient with acute myocardial infarction and subsequent ventricular tachycardia, cardiac arrest, resuscitation, and recovery is usually an emotionally charged event. Most physicians are able to recall exquisite details about that patient many years later.

In all likelihood, the explanatory models for knowledge stores in memory overlap, and the recall of relevant knowledge for reasoning is highly flexible and probably takes many forms (12).

Clinical Reasoning
As mentioned, cognitive research supports two primary pathways of clinical reasoning: analytic and nonanalytic (automatic) reasoning. Analytic reasoning is characterized as a conscious, deliberate process of activating knowledge stores, considering appropriate illness scripts, weighing relevant diagnostic hypotheses, considering probabilities, and making a judgment about the most likely explanation for a clinical presentation. As a conscious process, thinking about the quality of one's thinking (for example, "Am I considering all the diagnostic possibilities?") is accessible for reflection. Nonanalytic reasoning, on the other hand, is unconscious and rapid. Experienced clinicians are known to "just know" the diagnosis in some circumstances. Cognitive theory suggests that "just knowing" is a result of unconscious recognition of a set of clinical features that are encapsulated in memory and immediately recalled as a diagnosis, bypassing any effortful, conscious deliberation. This highly efficient process, called pattern recognition, is not accessible for reflection. One cannot consciously reconstruct and evaluate the unconscious process. The limitations of short-term working memory probably facilitate development of such efficient decision-making strategies that bypass consciousness.

The ability to recognize patterns and reason automatically results from extensive clinical experience. It follows that learners at the beginning of their clinical training will mostly use an analytic reasoning process. Over time, the frequently encountered clinical problems will be more easily recognized and the reasoning process will become more automatic.

Categorization of Clinical Problems
To efficiently recall relevant knowledge stores, physicians must be able to recognize what kind of problems they are trying to solve. Research on the role of problem definition in problem-solving suggests that transforming the patient's narrative and other clinical information into a synthesized abstraction, or problem representation, facilitates identification of the

problem category and activates the search, selection, and verification of the illness script (16).

The key to a successful problem representation is its level of abstraction. Problem summaries that retain unique features of the case at hand less often trigger illness scripts or cases stored in memory at a more abstract level. Often, the step of creating a problem representation occurs unconsciously (and is therefore presumed). When clinical problems are complex and filled with ambiguity, consciously creating a problem representation (for example, "So this is a case of an immunosuppressed man, with fever, weight loss, and dysphagia") can facilitate further relevant data gathering.

Developmental Frameworks
Schmidt and colleagues (17) proposed a staged theory of clinical reasoning, synthesized from research on novice–expert differences. Early learners use pathophysiologic explanations for clinical presentations, accessing knowledge stores organized by diseases. From clinical exposure, learners begin to recognize key features that define clinical syndromes, reorganizing stored medical knowledge into categories based on clinical presentation. Thus, the knowing and understanding of normal lung physiology and the pathologic changes that occur with pneumonia are stored in memory differently from the knowing and understanding of what it means when patients describe general malaise, fever, shaking chills, cough productive of purulent sputum, and difficulty breathing. Following clinical exposure to patients with pneumonia, this latter cluster of information triggers memory of experience with patients who had similar symptoms, their final diagnoses, and any learning through reading or discussion that occurred at that time.

Bordage and colleagues (18) focused on the discourse used in clinical reasoning. A categorization of discourse types emerged from this research, allowing the investigators to suggest that listening to physicians reason out loud about a clinical problem allows the observer to recognize the type of discourse organization, imply the underlying knowledge structures being used, and predict whether the physician is likely to come to the correct diagnosis. Box 1-2 describes 4 types of discourse organization.

Combined Strategies
Frequently, the most likely explanation for a patient's symptoms emerges readily and is retained as the diagnosis. For more complex problems, multiple hypotheses are plausible and additional diagnostic testing is performed in an effort to decrease uncertainty about the cause of the patient's symptoms. Although presented here as one of a series of steps, the entire

Box 1-2. Types of Discourse Organization

1. **Reduced.** Learners with little knowledge or understanding of the clinical problem cannot make connections between the features of the case and stored knowledge. Because knowledge is not triggered, it is impossible to distinguish absent knowledge from inaccessible knowledge. In response to the question, "What do you think about this problem?" the learner says very little of consequence, or essentially, "I don't know."

2. **Dispersed.** Learners with this type of discourse response to the question "What do you think?" talk about separate features of the case, which trigger associations with pathophysiology or diagnoses but fail to reflect consideration of other features and connect back to the case. Thus, the features present for a patient with pneumonia would be considered individually. Fever might trigger a list of diagnoses where fever is a prominent feature. Shortness of breath might trigger a whole new list of diagnoses where dyspnea is characteristic. Knowledge is abundant but the coherence provided by the clinical context of the case is ignored, yielding extensive diagnostic considerations without prioritization or any effort to make a plausible diagnosis.

3. **Elaborated.** This is characterized by the transformation of specific case features into abstract, synthesized terms. "I started feeling poorly a few days ago" becomes "acute," for example. These abstract descriptors, called semantic qualifiers, have two characteristics. They can easily be paired with an opposite quality: acute versus chronic; productive versus nonproductive cough; or ill-appearing versus well-appearing. Second, the descriptors most often fall into categories typically used to characterize the problem during the medical interview: *onset* ("When did your symptoms start?"—acute vs. subacute vs. chronic, sudden vs. gradual), *site* ("What is bothering you?"—unilateral vs. bilateral, localized vs. disseminated, monoarticular vs. polyarticular), *course* ("Do your symptoms come and go?"—episodic vs. continuous, recurrent vs. resolved), *severity* ("How would you describe your discomfort?"—severe vs. mild,

continued

Box 1-2. Types of Discourse Organization (continued)

sharp vs. dull), and *context* (young vs. older, male vs. female, smoker vs. nonsmoker). In addition, learners with elaborated discourse organization are actively comparing and contrasting diagnostic considerations with the features of the case. These oral presentations tend to be easy to follow and are well organized and concise.

4. **Compiled.** Clinical case discourse in this category tends to be brief and highly synthesized, and often extends beyond the available features, showing evidence of searching for elements missing from a well-developed understanding of the problem. Fewer diagnostic considerations are entertained. At first it may be difficult to distinguish a lucky guess or premature closure from compiled discourse organization. Upon further questioning ("Did you consider anything else as an explanation for his symptoms?"), the learner with compiled discourse organization can compare and contrast highly relevant diagnoses with the features of the case. Reduced and dispersed discourse organizations are associated with difficulty making an accurate diagnosis, but elaborated and compiled organizations are associated with diagnostic accuracy.

---

diagnostic reasoning process is better described as a collection of tasks adapted flexibly to the nature of the clinical problem. It is important that the diagnostician not get locked into one way of solving clinical problems. There are multiple mechanisms by which the clinician can arrive at the correct diagnosis. New evidence emerging from the cognitive research literature suggests that explicit instructions to use combined strategies or multiple approaches may be associated with higher diagnostic accuracy and may diminish susceptibility to unconscious reasoning biases. When Eva and colleagues (12) asked study participants to trust their intuition about the right diagnosis (automatic reasoning) and then check for presence (or absence) of key features (analytic reasoning), diagnostic accuracy improved. Further, when study participants were biased by a diagnostic suggestion that was incorrect, the use of combined automatic and analytic reasoning approaches yielded the highest diagnostic accuracy (12).

Little is known about the triggers that shift clinicians from automatic reasoning to analytic reasoning. Mamede and colleagues (19, 20), in a series of studies exploring the role of case complexity and perceived case difficulty, discovered that second-year internal medicine residents using analytic (reflective) reasoning more often came up with the correct diagnosis in clinical cases containing ambiguous features suggestive of more than one diagnosis or if they were biased by a suggestion that the case was difficult for others to solve. This line of inquiry suggests that case complexity may trigger an analytic approach to problem-solving, resulting in higher diagnostic accuracy. For trainees early in their clinical years, most cases are likely to be perceived as complex or ambiguous, reaffirming previous observations that novices tend to reason analytically.

Application

Cognitive theories provide the foundation for building knowledge stores in memory that facilitate timely and appropriate recall for use in diagnostic reasoning and clinical judgment. The exponential growth of medical knowledge easily overwhelms clinicians. Some evidence suggests that knowledge learned early on is more firmly anchored, requiring extra effort to revise and update. Systematic review of the medical literature is necessary to continually update memory stores and requires additional critical-reading skills. If reading about one's own patients bolsters memory related to clinical presentations and diagnoses, it follows that strong reading habits for continually updating one's memory with the best evidence for safe, effective, and beneficial care are required.

As experience accumulates, clinicians will increase their use of automatic (unconscious) reasoning in domains that are very familiar (21). One must build in habits of reflection to avoid premature closure and a keen eye for the unusual feature to be on a constant lookout for an unusual case masquerading as typical and familiar. Such habits are associated with expert performance in diagnostic reasoning (22).

Examples of Teaching Methods Grounded in Cognitive Theory

One-on-One Clinical Case Discussions

Typical of teaching in the ambulatory or emergency department settings, learners at all stages of training are usually required to present clinical cases to supervising preceptors. Questioning strategies, such as that outlined in the "One-Minute Preceptor" (23), can be used to engage learners to reason aloud about the clinical case, identify knowledge gaps, and compare and contrast a differential diagnosis list using features of the clinical case. These activities build and refine the learner's knowledge base, understanding, and judgment. Teaching in the examination room will probably help link key features of the patient's history and the physical examination with the illness scripts under consideration.

Teaching Rounds
With this approach, typical of teaching in the hospital setting, learners and teachers engage in group discussions about the patients on their service. These case discussions can be guided by questioning strategies, where lower-order questions are addressed to early learners (third-year medical students) and more complex, advanced questions are addressed to upper-level residents. Further, teachers can ask upper-level residents to answer questions raised by lower-level learners as a way of further solidifying understanding of concepts or discovering new knowledge gaps. Teaching at the bedside again reinforces the identification of key clinical features, linking them with new knowledge learned from the case discussion.

Clinical Case Conferences (Morning Report, Morbidity and Mortality Conference)
Although the learners may not be discussing clinical cases based on their own direct experience, these case conferences link clinical presentations with problem representations, key features, and an appropriate differential diagnosis (usually identifying and excluding far-fetched diagnostic hypotheses). These activities help build and refine illness scripts and categorical knowledge structures.

Collaborative Learning
Peer learners can facilitate improved knowledge and understanding for each other in a few different ways. In a peer-led discussion, one student presents a new case to other students in little chunks. A second student summarizes what he or she heard, providing an opportunity to give feedback to the first student about clarity of presentation. The second student lists anything he or she is thinking of as possible diagnoses. Then everyone in the group reviews each listed diagnosis, recalling the "textbook" version of what it will look like, linking book knowledge to the case. Students then vote on what percentage likelihood each diagnosis is assigned on the basis of knowledge of the case so far, adding up to 100% (tying in Bayesian reasoning). The first student then provides the next snippet of clinical information, repeating the same process, and watching how the percentage likelihoods change. Through discussion, students discover together what they know and what they don't know. The teacher's role in this case discussion method is to simply keep the students on track. Another approach includes having students trade case write-ups, asking for critique before handing in the write-up to

the supervising teacher or resident. Students learn from each other's patients and learn to provide constructive feedback in written form.

Self-Study

Independent reading and study builds knowledge and understanding. Learners should be taught the principles of evidence-based medicine to facilitate critical reading skills and attention to best evidence. Most often, early learners are still asking and answering background questions, so review articles and textbooks (or electronic sources such as Up-to-Date) are appropriate reading sources. More advanced learners who already have a strong foundational knowledge base will ask more foreground questions, and a focused literature search is appropriate. Learners should be encouraged to read about their own clinical cases, comparing and contrasting key and discriminating features for diagnostic considerations. A similar approach can be taken for diagnostic workups and management plans. Another method of self-study includes self-administered test and retest using multiple-choice questions, similar to those used in the American College of Physicians' Medical Knowledge and Self-Assessment Program. Learners should read to understand why a question was missed before retesting.

Clinical Case Write-ups

Learners should be encouraged to structure chart documentation that promotes linking of clinical learning with new knowledge. For example, the *assessment* portion of a clinical note should highlight the key features of the history, physical examination, laboratory testing, and imaging that support or refute a set of diagnostic hypotheses, tightly linking clinical reasoning to the features of the case. Box 1-3 outlines the implications for teachers that follow from cognitive learning theory.

❖ Social Learning Theory

Premise

Social learning theory assumes that relationships, interactions, and group dynamics have a powerful effect on learning.

Overview

Social learning theories emerged in response to perceived difficulties that cognitive and behavioral theories have in explaining learning from social interactions, and are sometimes seen as a bridge between the two. People learn from one another in social contexts, and this includes imitation and modeling. Social learning theories accept that the environment influences

Box 1-3. Cognitive Theory: Implications for Teachers

▶ Cognitive learning theory is best used to guide learning when trying to build useful knowledge structures and teach clinical reasoning.

▶ This theory suggests that *experience* with clinical cases is crucial for organizing knowledge in memory and facilitating recall. This implies that teachers should 1) be mindful of the learner's prior clinical experiences before making judgments about performance and 2) facilitate recall of prior experiences during clinical case discussions.

▶ Teachers should expose early learners to *typical cases* with guided reading plans to facilitate development of strong anchor prototypes. Subsequent case exposure can be related back to the learner's understanding of these anchor cases, using a compare-and-contrast strategy.

▶ Teachers should encourage learners to actively *identify the problem* they are trying to solve, using abstract problem representations, especially for complex clinical syndromes with ambiguity. Formulating the case at this abstract level facilitates connections to scripts and prototypes.

▶ Teachers should encourage learners to use a *compare-and-contrast* strategy when reading about clinical presentations. Specifically, even after the final diagnosis is known, learners should select at least two of the leading diagnostic hypotheses and read about them, comparing and contrasting clinical presentation, physical examination findings, and laboratory and imaging results, all in an effort to learn (and be able to recall) key and discriminating features for the diagnoses under consideration.

▶ Teachers should listen to learners reasoning out loud (in response to variations on the question, "What do you think is going on here?"). The type of discourse used may be a clue to the learner's understanding of the case and correctness of the diagnosis being entertained.

▶ Teachers should encourage case write-ups that demonstrate comparing and contrasting of key and discriminating clinical features in justifying the selection of a working diagnosis among the most likely candidate diagnoses.

behavior, but add that behavior reciprocally changes the environment. Authority is granted to the social group, which determines the values and norms for social behaviors. The emotional and social tone of the learning situation strongly influences the student's motivation and learning.

Background

Early work in developmental psychology focused on strong interactions between cultural norms, cognitive patterns, and observable behaviors. This led to an appreciation of the importance of symbols, or objects with particular cultural and historical significance. These symbols—a judge's robe, a doctor's white coat, a police officer's badge—become place holders for identity and social roles, and come with special privileges and obligations that are culturally derived. Our training environments are replete with symbols. Look around. Can you tell what job each employee has by the uniform and paraphernalia? Many times our symbols reflect our values, even if we are unaware of that fact. How welcoming and understandable is the signage around your hospital or clinic for a newcomer? What values are reflected (or ignored) in the orientation materials for your rotation? Social learning theories warn us to align the symbols in our learning environments with our core values as much as possible.

The other key element in social learning is human interaction. Social scientists have identified reciprocal determinism (the environment and the person determine each other) as an important factor in many learning situations. Emotions tend to be reproduced and amplified through interactions. With planning, this can be explicitly exploited (warmly greet your new student) or resisted (avoid reacting in anger to a frustrated outburst from a harried resident). Social learning theories invite us to reflect and improve on our interactions as teachers. We are in positions of power and influence and, for better or worse, we become role models for learners. For instance, one of the best predictors of student hand-washing between patients is faculty hand-washing between patients.

Another social learning influence is reflected in the concept of "zone of proximal development." Simply stated, this is the difference between what learners can master on their own versus what they can master with peers or a knowledgeable mentor (24). In contrast to the "teacher as authority" in behavioral theory, the role of the teacher in social learning is to give hints, provide organizing structure, summarize, and identify critical elements to help a learner, or a group of learners, manipulate ideas to create shared understandings and to achieve greater mastery.

As an example, consider a student who observes a patient get very angry at her resident about a delay in discharge. The student knows this is outside of the resident's control. In one learning environment, the resident remains calm and apologizes for the problem, and the patient calms down. The student asks the resident how she avoids bristling when being unfairly attacked. The resident says, "I've learned to pay attention to my own feelings. Anger is my red flag that I need to slow down. After all, how do you feel during unexpected delays? I realized that the patient was angry at the delay, not me." The student admires this resident. In the future, trading her own white jacket in for the long white coat of a senior resident may help her literally and figuratively adopt this role of equanimity in difficult situations.

In another situation, an overworked resident may bark back at the patient. She may describe him on attending rounds as demanding, and she and the attending may share a few choice epithets, calling the patient a "crock" or "pain in the behind." They may go on to grumble about how "this kind of patient is what makes medicine difficult." What is the student learning in this environment?

Lave and Wenger (25, 26) have built on these concepts, observing that participation in local social systems or "communities of practice" is a fundamental process by which learning occurs (Box 1-4). Within that community, members negotiate meaning by participating in real activity (commensurate with their current skill level) and helping to make concrete and visible the successful social practices and products. The ward team members, for example, share the goal of caring for the patients assigned to their team, expect everyone to participate fairly, assign responsibilities based on level of training, and share in the success of a job well done (like the first resident in the example above). On the other hand, a poorly functioning team may result in unsuccessful negotiation of goals, unevenly assigned responsibilities, and failure to communicate effectively. Medical students on these teams often struggle to find meaningful participation in the real work of caring for patients. Individuals, not the group, take credit for success and may blame others for failure (like the second resident and attending in the example above).

There is always tension between the roles that the group requires and the identity that the individual experiences as "self." This tension is stabi-

Box 1-4. Three Elements of Communities of Practice

1. Mutual engagement
2. Joint enterprise or goal
3. Shared menu of actions for achieving that goal

lized through local conversations and narrative patterns in the group. Concrete products such as rules, roles, and objects become placeholders around which the community can organize its actions. For instance, medical students may be trained to draw blood but don't do so in a particular clinic because "they never have before." After discussion at a team meeting, there may be general consensus that the students could draw blood. A new policy document (placeholder) makes this permission concrete, defines the conditions when it can occur, and facilitates future interactions around blood draws. Communities of practice are spontaneous, organic, and informal. They are based on the sharing of knowledge and the expansion of expertise, and they resist supervision and interference from the outside (27).

There is a natural progression in these communities (Figure 1-1). Newcomers can see only written documents and other placeholders. Once they are accepted as legitimate members, they participate in the practice of the community, contributing to the community's product. During this time they may experience discrepancies between what the community says and what the community does. In the second example in the preceding discussion, this would occur if the orientation manual had a stated goal of respecting patients, while the observed behavior of the second resident and faculty member contradicted that. Later, as "old timers," they become part of the core of the community that sets and modifies core values, and at this time they have the opportunity to address these discrepancies. With each new entering group of residents and departing group of residency graduates, the members of the community of practice within a given training

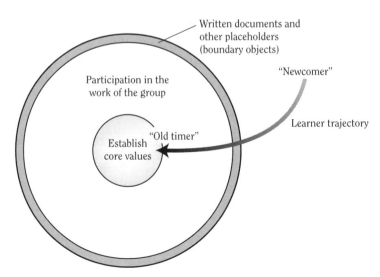

Figure 1-1 The community of practice learning model with a typical learner trajectory.

program change. The intern newcomers negotiate membership in the community and begin to influence the group's values through disruptive change. Each new intern brings his or her own experiences and learned expectations from medical school experiences. Shared understanding of the meaning of expectations and behaviors, including the language used to describe rules and expectations, must be renegotiated. As a result, the entire group evolves. The teacher's role is to be fully aware of this acculturation process, both the impact of new members disrupting existing norms and the support newcomers need, assisting them in negotiating membership in the community. In essence, the teacher lives at the interface between communities of practice, assisting newcomers with their transition from their prior communities to their new communities.

Many serious learning problems are failures of this acculturation process. Some learners fail to find a role in this community of practice, remain isolated and excluded, and choose to change specialties or leave training altogether. Others fail to progress as expected, such as when an intern cannot function independently by the end of the year and cannot be promoted to the next training level.

Other research paradigms have shifted the unit of analysis subtly from the learner to the system as a whole (28). In these theories, there is a complex relational web that connects the individual person, the community, and the object of activity (such as caring for patients). The community exerts control over the individual by the tools it provides and through rules, norms, and division of labor. In our example, the performance of the second resident may have more to do with expected workload, lack of realistic communication training, and a dysfunctional discharge process than personal failings. These theories suggest that we should attend to our system during disturbances. Disturbance reveals elements that are usually tacit, making them available for conscious reflection and improvement. Moreover, we should not simply write off concerns from low-power members of our community (patients and students) as uninformed or naive. They may have the freshest eyes to see engrained bad habits (Box 1-5).

Application

Social theories provide the foundation for a great deal of what happens in the clinical arena, and they have a particularly direct application for professionalism education and understanding the "hidden curriculum." Professionalism is taught through expectations, experiences, and evaluations (29). Expectations are communicated formally via orientation sessions, policies, and procedures (boundary objects). As seen in Figure 1-1, it is important for the group to continually align these boundary objects with

Box 1-5. Key Aspects of Social Learning Theory

▶ A social learning community provides trainee roles that make meaningful contributions to the work products of the group and are commensurate with knowledge and skills at any given developmental level (e.g., student blood drawing in the emergency department).

▶ A social learning community strives to "live" its core values. These may be explicit (e.g., exam tray ready to facilitate women's health) or implicit (e.g., a welcoming feel toward new learners). Nonetheless, the mismatch between what we say and what we do is frequently glaring, leads to cynicism, and contributes to countervalue learning and degradation of professionalism.

▶ People exert effects on each other as they interact. Teachers should model appropriate behaviors, avoid inappropriate behavior, and be sensitive to the process of acculturation, which is central to the community and all its participants.

▶ The social learning community should be structured to build self-efficacy in learners: allowing them to have incremental success, providing accurate and supportive feedback, and exposing them to successful peer performances.

▶ A social learning community encourages learners' comments and involvement.

core values. This is an ongoing process. Experiences may include patient–doctor courses, ethics lectures, parables, and explicit role modeling. Social learning theory emphasizes incremental authentic roles commensurate with knowledge and skills. Faculty should provide scaffolding and guidance, and be available as role models. For instance, formal ethics teaching could be accomplished for early learners by lectures and exposure to a mock ethics committee. Later, intermediate learners could have support roles on the actual ethics committee and time for guided reflection and discussion. Advanced learners could have representation on the ethics committee. Professionalism evaluation, based on social learning theory, should capture learner performance on relevant tasks in real-world contexts from multiple perspectives.

The "hidden curriculum" refers to all the ways that informal learning takes place beyond the lecture, laboratory, clinic, and ward—including the joke that is told in the elevator, the example set at the isolation patient's door, and the stories over lunch about entertaining misperceptions (30). Try walking through your teaching venue with the eyes of a newcomer. What do you see: Signage that is tasteful and helpful or haphazard and blunt? Interaction that is quiet and respectful or loud and abrasive? What do you hear: conversations that sound businesslike or confidential information? Norms are being transmitted and things are being learned, whether we intend them or not.

Examples of Teaching Methods Grounded in Social Learning Theory

Critical Incident Reports

Critical incident reports are short narratives in which learners write about their own memorable and influential learning experiences. These are usually discussed in small groups with trusted faculty mentors. They may be open-ended or directed (for example, "Write about a difficult patient"). The technique can reveal deep insights for learners and faculty, such as the tension between empathy and acculturation (31). It can also reveal hidden assumptions, such as what behaviors indicate good teamwork (32). Care must be taken ahead of time to identify structures for dealing with unexpected information (such as unprofessional faculty behavior that is revealed).

Journaling

Keeping a journal while undergoing the role and identity transitions involved in medical education can be a valuable reflective exercise. Teacher commentary is important and can be informal, providing a safe place to question values and beliefs (33), or very formal, such as using qualitative analysis to identify key factors and constructs that affect the development of attitudes and professionalism (34).

Multisource (360°) Feedback

Multisource feedback, also known as 360° feedback, is a questionnaire-based assessment method using evaluation by peers, patients, and coworkers. The process is resource intensive but has the potential to change performance and facilitate personal development (35). Questionnaires must be tested to assure adequate psychometric properties. Both raters and recipients must be oriented to the purpose and the instruments. Feedback is received in the form of aggregate ratings and mean peer ratings. A mentor usually presents the feedback and helps the recipient to process the feedback, foster reflection, and create an action plan. Box 1-6 outlines implications for teachers that derive from social learning theory.

Box 1-6. Social Learning Theory: Implications for Teachers

▶ Social learning theory is best used to guide learning when trying to teach attitudes or values.

▶ It suggests that teachers should be aware of their situational power, both as role models (being careful how we behave) and as authorities (being careful not to overwhelm or intimidate the learner). Social learning problems are always an opportunity to first reflect on ourselves as role models.

▶ It further suggests we should attend carefully to roles, so that they are meaningful and appropriate to the learning level, and to relationships, so that they provide challenge, respect, and support.

▶ Social teaching points should be based on a shared core value.

❖ Learning From Experience

Premise
Experiential learning theory assumes that learning is based in concrete experiences augmented by reflection, generalization, and concept testing.

> *Tell me, and I will forget. Show me, and I may remember. Involve me, and I will understand.*
> — *Confucius, circa 450 BC*

Overview
In the early 20th century, a radical new approach to learning developed that deemphasized lectures and abstract facts (knowing *what*) and focused more on experience and practical knowledge (knowing *how*). By the 1980s, this was formalized into "experiential learning theory," with its cycle of concrete experience → reflective observation → abstract conceptualization → active experimentation. The learning cycle includes aspects of the previous theories and can be especially useful for organizing medical training experiences.

Background
In the early 20th century, the Chicago "pragmatist" revolt in education, sociology, and philosophy, espoused most clearly by America's preeminent

philosopher of education, John Dewey, challenged long-held views of knowledge and learning. Educators espoused a "progressive" approach to learning, based on experience, in direct contradiction to the traditional approach of that time, learning from texts and teachers. Dewey emphasized that "one's current experience is a function of the interaction between one's past experiences and the present situation." He saw a critical need to attend to the current learning environment and context (a social perspective), as well as how to connect new information to prior concepts (a cognitive perspective).

From this and other schools of thought, Kolb (36) developed his influential experiential learning theory. This theory is captured in a recurrent cycle (Figure 1-2).

Reflection is a critical step in this cycle. It lays the ground work for intentional action (as opposed to reflexive actions) in the next similar situation. Reflection can be part of planning, may occur in the midst of action and decision-making, or may happen after action when there is time for deliberate analysis and inquiry. Priming the learner (behavioral) can encourage and focus reflection before the experience—for example, saying "I want you to see this next patient and pay attention to what emotions you feel during the encounter." Reflective questions after the encounter work

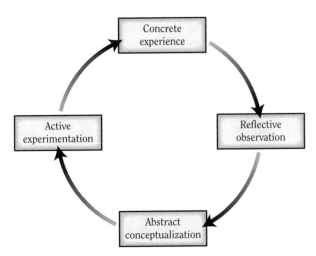

Figure 1-2 The recurrent cycle of concrete experience (patient encounter), reflective observation (attending to that encounter as it unfolds), abstract conceptualization (forming a generalization from that encounter), and active experimentation (testing that generalization in the next similar encounter). Experiential learning theory shifts the role of the clinical teacher from that of a purveyor of information to that of a facilitator of learning.

well for early learners—for instance, "How well do you think the treatment is working?" (cognitive). The capacity to reflect-in-action (during the encounter) and change strategies on the fly is the mark of a seasoned professional (37). Teachers can promote this level of professional performance by sharing their own reflections (social) as they and the learner are mutually engaged in clinical problem-solving.

Application
Experiential learning theory is informed by the other three foundational theories: behavioral, cognitive, and social learning theories. At each stage of the experiential learning cycle, each of the foundation theories guides the learning process.

Selecting Experiences
Assuming that experience with patients is the medium for clinical learning, careful attention must be paid to the settings and types of experiences we are providing for learners. Behavioral theories remind us to examine the skills and competencies we intend to improve with this component and assure that necessary elements are available. For example, if a curricular goal is patient communication, we must assure that learners have sufficient opportunity and time to converse with patients. It may be important that some of these conversations are observed by faculty (a resource issue) who have skills in evaluation and feedback (a faculty development issue). Cognitive learning theory suggests that we attend to case mix to assure that the types of illnesses outlined in curricular goals are likely to be seen. For instance, if we are going to test learners about management of congestive heart failure, we must be sure that they are likely to see such patients or have appropriate substitute experiences. Some selection of patients is appropriate in early training to assure that the depth and complexity of the patient match the developmental level of the learner. By the end of training, residents should be encouraged to handle the responsibility of a full, unselected panel of patients. Social learning theory suggests that experiences should be designed so that learners are making meaningful contributions to the group's product. It is also important to select learning sites with clinical teachers who are enthusiastic and committed.

Facilitating Reflective Observation
Reflective observation involves viewing a new experience through the interpretive lens of experience, current readings, or the organizing framework of a clinical teacher. Behavioral approaches to reflection focus on a particular skill (for example, active listening). Early learners begin with reflection-on-action (after the encounter) by asking themselves how well

their behaviors worked and why. More advanced learners can be explicitly encouraged to reflect-in-action by asking them to "be the fly on the wall," and watching their behaviors and modifying them even as they participate in the interview. Cognitive theories suggest that similar exercises should focus on the effectiveness of concepts and models of illness. Social theories remind us that preceptors, by virtue of their greater experience, can focus on critical elements of the upcoming encounter in a way that will assist reflection. The preceptor's experience provides knowledge of the common stumbling blocks and leverage points, and sets the stage for skillful questioning after the encounter about the behaviors, concepts, or emotions that were observed or occurred during the encounter, thereby promoting reflection and, ultimately, insight and learning.

Encouraging Conceptual Thinking
Learning and constructing generalizations from specific situations can be enhanced by role modeling (social), seeing the consequences of ones actions (behavioral), and engaging in inquiry (cognitive). Over time, the process of generalizing from many cases reorganizes knowledge in memory into highly efficient and effective structures. Behavioral approaches to concept formation focus on skills such as information acquisition, critical literature review, and logical argument. Cognitive theories suggest that discussion of alternative perspectives and encouraging independent reading with active comparisons to one's existing knowledge can broaden conceptual models and connections. Social learning theories remind us that we can role-model active conceptualization by thinking aloud and providing rationale for suggested actions. Clinical teachers who are enthusiastic, respectful, and self-disclosing can also promote conceptual thinking by sharing uncertainty and role modeling inquiry.

Supporting Active Experimentation
The final step in experiential learning is to test the validity of the insights gained from previous cases by applying them to new cases and examining the results. To achieve this, it is important to have several exposures to common or important illnesses. Continuity of patient care increases the likelihood that learners will observe the natural progression of illness and the effects of clinical decisions. Clinical teachers need to observe important behaviors. This may be difficult to accomplish but is critical to coaching on communication or physical examination skills. Concepts are improved by feedback that is descriptive, specific, and timely. This should be linked to explicit goals and, if it is corrective feedback, should include suggestions for improvement and an action plan. As learners advance, the amount, types, and sources of feedback (such as peer, staff, and patient feedback)

should increase. Clinical teachers who are stimulating, respectful, self-disclosing, and nonjudgmental can establish a social milieu where the risk-taking involved in experiential learning is safer (38).

Examples of Teaching Methods Grounded in Experiential Learning Theory

Patient Care–Based Rotations

For third-year medical students, any rotation that includes students in the active, hands-on assessment of patients, discussion of clinical problems, and management decisions and actions involves experiential learning. In graduate medical education, nearly all learning activities are experiential, supported by conferences or didactic learning. In each case, assigning learners to assess, diagnose, and manage patients provides concrete experiences. The extent to which reflection in or on action, abstract conceptualization, and active application of learning to the next similar patient takes place will depend on the structure of the teaching activities associated with clinical rotations. If, for example, a clinical teacher supervising a group of learners for a 2-week hospital-based rotation systematically sets aside some time each week to reflect formally on the team's patient care experiences, assisting the team with identifying general concepts learned in the act of delivering patient care and how the approach might be modified for future encounters, the full value of learning from experience is realized.

Morbidity and Mortality Conference

These conferences are designed to foster learning from peer and expert review of errors and complications in patient care. Newer versions use quality techniques such as root cause analysis (39) or standardized data-collection and -reporting formats that allow error profile analysis and interinstitutional comparisons (40).

Videotape Review of Clinical Encounters

Videotape review has a distinct advantage over observation with feedback because it can help transcend defensive rationalizations such as "I didn't really do it that way, it was just their misperception." Videotape with faculty review has demonstrated performance improvements in health supervision examinations for pediatric residents (41). Videotape review can also be self-assessed by the learner using a checklist form without faculty review (42).

Normative Clinical Performance Reports

Guideline-based performance data can be provided to learners and compared with normative or target standards. This usually requires an electronic medical record system and works best with "full-denominator" data (for example, based on all diabetic patients in the practice, not just a chart review of a few of those patients). Care must be taken to ensure that the patient registry is accurate. Clinical performance data can be incorporated into a comprehensive chronic disease management program that improves process and clinical outcomes (43) (Box 1-7).

Box 1-7. Experiential Learning Theory: Implications for Teachers

- ► Experiential learning theory is ideally suited for situations in which reflection and conceptualization are most important for learning.
- ► Experiential learning theory warrants that we provide time and resources to support this reflection, conceptualization, and generalizations from patient care.
- ► Experiential learning theory underscores the importance of patient continuity, where the learner can test the validity of concepts derived from early patient care with that patient over time.

REFERENCES

1. **Dick W, Carey L.** The Systematic Design of Instruction. Glenview, IL: Scott, Foresman; 1978.
2. **Barrows HS.** An overview of the uses of standardized patients for teaching and evaluating clinical skills. AAMC. Acad Med. 1993;68:443-51; discussion 451-3.
3. **Harden RM, Stevenson M, Downie WW, Wilson GM.** Assessment of clinical competence using objective structured examination. Br Med J. 1975;1:447-51.
4. **Accreditation Council for Graduate Medical Education.** Frequently asked questions. Accessed at www.acgme.org.
5. **American Association of Medical Colleges.** Report 1: Learning objectives for medical student education. Guidelines for Medical Schools. Medical School Objectives Project. Washington, DC: American Association of Medical Colleges; 1998.,
6. **Harden RM, Crosby JR, Davis MH, Friedman M.** From Competency to Meta-Competency: A Model for the Specification of Learning Outcomes. Dundee, United Kingdom: Association for Medical Education in Europe; 1999.
7. **CanMEDS 2000 Project Societal Needs Working Group.** CanMEDS 2000: Extract from the CanMEDS 2000 Project Societal Needs Working Group Report. Medical Teacher. 2000;22:549-54.
8. **Wayne DB, Butter J, Siddall VJ, Fudala MJ, Wade LD, Feinglass J, et al.** Mastery learning of advanced cardiac life support skills by internal medicine residents using simulation technology and deliberate practice. J Gen Intern Med. 2006;21:251-6.

9. **Newble D.** Techniques for measuring clinical competence: objective structured clinical examinations. Med Educ. 2004;38:199-203.

10. **Elstein AS, Schwartz A, Schwarz A.** Clinical problem solving and diagnostic decision making: selective review of the cognitive literature. BMJ. 2002;324:729-32.

11. **Norman G.** Research in clinical reasoning: past history and current trends. Med Educ. 2005;39:418-27.

12. **Eva KW, Hatala RM, Leblanc VR, Brooks LR.** Teaching from the clinical reasoning literature: combined reasoning strategies help novice diagnosticians overcome misleading information. Med Educ. 2007;41:1152-8.

13. **Charlin B, Boshuizen HP, Custers EJ, Feltovich PJ.** Scripts and clinical reasoning. Med Educ. 2007;41:1178-84.

14. **Schmidt HG, Rikers RM.** How expertise develops in medicine: knowledge encapsulation and illness script formation. Med Educ. 2007;41:1133-9.

15. **Custers EJ, Regehr G, Norman GR.** Mental representations of medical diagnostic knowledge: a review. Acad Med. 1996;71:S55-61.

16. **Chang RW, Bordage G, Connell KJ.** The importance of early problem representation during case presentations. Acad Med. 1998;73:S109-11.

17. **Schmidt HG, Norman GR, Boshuizen HP.** A cognitive perspective on medical expertise: theory and implication. Acad Med. 1990;65:611-21.

18. **Bordage G.** Elaborated knowledge: a key to successful diagnostic thinking. Acad Med. 1994;69:883-5.

19. **Mamede S, Schmidt HG, Rikers RM, Penaforte JC, Coelho-Filho JM.** Breaking down automaticity: case ambiguity and the shift to reflective approaches in clinical reasoning. Med Educ. 2007;41:1185-92.

20. **Mamede S, Schmidt HG, Rikers RM, Penaforte JC, Coelho-Filho JM.** Influence of perceived difficulty of cases on physicians' diagnostic reasoning. Acad Med. 2008;83:1210-6.

21. **Norman G, Young M, Brooks L.** Non-analytical models of clinical reasoning: the role of experience. Med Educ. 2007;41:1140-5.

22. **Moulton CA, Regehr G, Mylopoulos M, MacRae HM.** Slowing down when you should: a new model of expert judgment. Acad Med. 2007;82:S109-16.

23. **Neher JO, Gordon KC, Meyer B, Stevens N.** A five-step "microskills" model of clinical teaching. J Am Board Fam Pract. 1992;5:419-24.

24. **Vygotsky LS.** Mind in Society. Cambridge, MA: Harvard Univ Pr; 1978.

25. **Lave J, Wenger E.** Situated Learning. Legitimate Peripheral Participation. Cambridge, United Kingdom: Cambridge Univ Pr; 1991.

26. **Wenger E.** Communities of Practice. Learning, Meaning, and Identity. Cambridge, United Kingdom: Cambridge Univ Pr; 1998.

27. **Wenger EC, Snyder WM.** Communities of practice: the organizational frontier. Harvard Business Review. 2000;Jan-Feb:139-45.

28. **Engström Y.** Expansive visibilization of work: an activity-theoretical perspective. Computer-Supported Cooperative Work. 1999;8:63-93.

29. **Stern DT, Papadakis M.** The developing physician—becoming a professional. N Engl J Med. 2006;355:1794-9.

30. **Hafferty FW, Franks R.** The hidden curriculum, ethics teaching, and the structure of medical education. Acad Med. 1994;69:861-71.

31. **Branch W, Pels RJ, Lawrence RS, Arky R.** Becoming a doctor. Critical-incident reports from third-year medical students. N Engl J Med. 1993;329:1130-2.

32. **Hill-Sakurai LE, Lee CA, Schickedanz A, Maa J, Lai CJ.** A professional development course for the clinical clerkships: developing a student-centered curriculum. J Gen Intern Med. 2008;23:964-8.
33. **Ashbury JE, Fletcher BM, Birtwhistle RV.** Personal journal writing in a communication skills course for first-year medical students. Med Educ. 1993;27:196-204.
34. **Ballon BC, Skinner W.** "Attitude is a little thing that makes a big difference": reflection techniques for addiction psychiatry training. Acad Psychiatry. 2008;32:218-24.
35. **Lockyer J.** Multisource feedback in the assessment of physician competencies. J Contin Educ Health Prof. 2003;23:4-12.
36. **Kolb DA.** Experiential learning. Experience as the Source of Learning and Development. Englewood Cliffs, NJ: Prentice Hall; 1984.
37. **Schön DA.** The Reflective Practitioner: How Professionals Think in Action. New York: Basic Books; 1983.
38. **Skeff KM, Stratos GA, Berman J, Bergen MR.** Improving clinical teaching. Evaluation of a national dissemination program. Arch Intern Med. 1992;152:1156-61.
39. **Bechtold ML, Scott S, Dellsperger KC, Hall LW, Nelson K, Cox KR.** Educational quality improvement report: outcomes from a revised morbidity and mortality format that emphasised patient safety. Postgrad Med J. 2008;84:211-6.
40. **Antonacci AC, Lam S, Lavarias V, Homel P, Eavey RA.** A report card system using error profile analysis and concurrent morbidity and mortality review: surgical outcome analysis, part II. J Surg Res. 2009;153:95-104.
41. **McCormick DP, Rassin GM, Stroup-Benham CA, Baldwin CD, Levine HG, Persaud DI, et al.** Use of videotaping to evaluate pediatric resident performance of health supervision examinations of infants. Pediatrics. 1993;92:116-20.
42. **Zick A, Granieri M, Makoul G.** First-year medical students' assessment of their own communication skills: a video-based, open-ended approach. Patient Educ Couns. 2007;68:161-6.
43. **DiPiero A, Dorr DA, Kelso C, Bowen JL.** Integrating systematic chronic care for diabetes into an academic general internal medicine resident-faculty practice. J Gen Intern Med. 2008;23:1749-56.

2

Applying Theory to Educational Practice

C. Scott Smith, MD, FACP
Judith L. Bowen, MD, FACP

Often the best approach to understanding how theories of learning can help faculty diagnose and respond to teaching challenges in clinical settings is to study cases that represent familiar circumstances for teachers. The following cases, or vignettes, illustrate problems addressed from the perspective of a simple theoretical frame (vignettes 1 to 9) or multiple theoretical frames (vignettes 10 to 12), in which theories are contrasted and often found to be complementary. In general, when clinical teachers face teaching challenges related to knowledge, a cognitive frame works best; when the problem is one of skills, a behavioral frame works best; and when the challenge is an attitude problem, a social frame is most appropriate. Most clinical learning takes place in clinical settings, raising the possibility that the experiential learning frame will frequently apply, especially when reflection seems appropriate.

The cases are organized developmentally, starting with medical students and ending with senior internal medicine residents. Vignettes 1, 2, 10, 11, and 12 are situated in ambulatory settings. The others represent teaching challenges in hospital settings. In each case, the learning challenge is identified and the manner in which the theoretical frames can be applied to help determine teachers' possible responses to the challenge at hand are described (Table 2-1).

KEY POINTS
- Start by identifying and labeling the teaching problem or learner difficulty.
- Learn to anticipate common problems during transitions (such as the first ward rotation for students or the management and leadership role of a new senior resident).
- Learner difficulties always provide an opportunity for the teacher to reflect first on the training experience: Is the orientation to this rotation clear and complete? Are we role-modeling appropriate values and behaviors?
- Teaching problems or learner difficulties are often complex, and more than one learning theory might apply; the selection of an approach based on one theory often involves tradeoffs.
- Teaching strategies for complex problems may require a combined or staged approach to address the learner difficulty.

❖ Vignette 1: Disorganized Case Presentation

A third-year student new to his outpatient rotation is presenting a partner's patient who is undergoing chemotherapy for a myeloproliferative disease. The patient presented to the office today with a red, swollen great toe on his right foot and a low-grade fever.

> **Student presentation:** *"The patient has a sore, red, warm right first toe for 3 days that is getting worse. He now rates the pain as 8 out of 10. His mother had diabetes and his aunt had coronary disease. He currently takes prednisone and prochlorperazine. The toe feels better when he elevates the leg. He has had some nausea and emesis, but mainly with chemotherapy. Oh yeah, he has some sort of bone marrow cancer. He has no known allergies. His last treatment was 1 week ago and he received antithymocyte globulin and cyclosporine. He has had a mild subjective fever but does not have a thermometer. He denies chills or diaphoresis. His temperature is 99.9°F. He doesn't have any inguinal nodes. No one else in his family is sick or has a rash. He had a similar pain once after he broke his toe playing soccer, but he hasn't had any trauma this time. On exam the right first toe is very swollen, warm, red, and exquisitely tender. The other foot is normal. His blood pressure is 128/73 and his pulse is 78. No one in his family has*

ever had arthritis. I'm not sure what is causing this since he has had not trauma. What would you like me to order?"

The problem the teacher must address in this situation is the long, disorganized case presentation that is inappropriate for the ambulatory set-

Table 2-1. Summary of Vignettes and Teaching Challenges

Vignette	Title	Teaching Challenge	Theoretical Approach
1	Disorganized case presentation	Addressing a long, disorganized case presentation	Behavioral
2	Missed diagnosis	Making a commitment to a diagnostic hypothesis	Cognitive
3	Priorities on teaching rounds	Preserving meaningful participation for learners in the setting of electronic health records	Social
4	Student transition to clinical learning	Supporting the transition from learning in the classroom to learning from patient care	Experiential
5	Failure to appreciate illness severity	Addressing failure to appreciate severe illness	Experiential
6	An evolving clinical syndrome	Providing cognitive feedback	Cognitive
7	Team management trouble	Assisting with a team management strategy	Behavioral
8	Making time to teach	Helping the resident new to the teaching role	Experiential
9	Overlooked complexity	Addressing resident's failure to recognize clinical uncertainty	Cognitive
10	Delinquent charting	Exploring the relationship between delinquent charting, teamwork, and patient safety	Behavioral, social
11	Decision-making within a hospital system	Addressing the hierarchical conflict that may be interfering with decision-making	Cognitive, social
12	The busy resident	Addressing a professionalism issue	Behavioral, social

ting. Failure to follow a structured protocol or set of rules (that is, the skill of case presentation) suggests that a behavioral theoretical response may be helpful.

From the behavioral theory perspective, the student demonstrates a low competency performance for the expectation of delivering organized case presentations (1). Remember that the behavioral perspective focuses on mastery of concrete, objective, measurable behaviors. Hypotheses explaining why a student is not meeting a performance goal include those outlined in Table 1-1 in chapter 1. If the assumption is that this new student has had experience with presenting cases, the next hypothesis to consider is that he may not understand what is expected, particularly in the office setting. So this would be an appropriate opportunity to make sure that orientation materials for the rotation contain specific guidelines for presentation, and to review these guidelines with the student (2). For example, the preceptor might say,

> **Preceptor:** *I'm pleased that you were able to obtain all the important elements of the history in this case. However, we get very busy in the office setting and it will benefit you in the long run to work on organizing your case presentations to help us work efficiently together in this setting. I would like you to focus on three things in your presentations. First, they have to be two minutes long or less. You should practice and time them until you get the hang of that. Second, they need to be in a specific order: a chronological history of present illness; pertinent past, family, and social history; all the vital signs; and then pertinent physical findings. You may want to organize your notes in that order until this becomes more routine. Finally, I want you in each case to commit to a diagnosis and a plan. It doesn't have to be right, but it will help you synthesize the story and make better plans.*

This type of feedback provides the student with clear expectations for case presentations in the ambulatory setting. It may not be all that is required, but it is an appropriate place to start.

❖ Vignette 2: Missed Diagnosis

A third-year student is presenting a case to his outpatient preceptor. The patient was scheduled for an urgent care visit after calling to report a fever and cough.

> **Student presentation:** *Our next patient is a 69-year-old man who developed a cough and shortness of breath. He was in his usual*

state of health until yesterday, when he awoke in the morning with chills, sweating, and a cough. He took some Tylenol, drank fluids, and rested, but he felt generally achy all day. Today, he noted some shortness of breath, so he called for this appointment. He denies orthopnea, but his cough kept him awake part of the night last night. No hemoptysis or chest pain. He thinks his symptoms are a bit worse with activity. His past history is notable only for diabetes type 2, which is well controlled on glipizide. He is married, lives with his wife. They don't have any pets. They have not traveled anywhere in the past 3 months. On physical exam, his temperature is 38.5°C, blood pressure is 110/60, pulse is 110, and respiratory rate is 22. When I listen to his lungs, he has some crackles at both bases, not much else. His heart exam is normal except for tachycardia, and his abdomen and extremities are normal. I think he needs an electrocardiogram but I'm not sure what else.

The problem the teacher must address in this situation is that the student failed to appreciate the clinical diagnosis. Concern about a learner's ability to synthesize a case suggests that a cognitive theoretical approach will be helpful.

From a cognitive theory perspective, the student seems to have trouble identifying the key features in this case that point to the diagnosis of community-acquired pneumonia. The quality and structure of the case presentation suggest that he may have a better knowledge base than he is demonstrating (3). He may simply have trouble accessing his knowledge base. He may also not have a clear idea of what type of problem he is trying to solve (4).

The preceptor should have the student formulate a problem representation, connect this case to prior experiences of similar cases, and then identify two plausible diagnostic hypotheses. For example, the preceptor might first say "Can you sum up this case in one sentence for me?" If the student struggles to respond, the preceptor should suggest her own problem representation: "An older man with the acute onset of fever, cough, malaise, and worrisome vital signs." Once the student and preceptor agree on the type of problem they are trying to solve—the problem representation—then the preceptor should ask "Have you ever seen a case like this before?" If the student acknowledges prior experience with this problem type, the preceptor should ask, "What was the first diagnosis that came to mind when you heard 'fever, cough, and general malaise'?" Additional questions one can ask might include: "How is this case similar to or different from other similar cases you have seen? What other things popped into your mind?" This teaching strategy activates the student's stored knowledge, making it more readily available for application to the current case

(5). The student may now be ready and willing to propose a diagnosis and plan of action. The preceptor should encourage the student to identify a plausible diagnosis and one reasonable alternative. For example, in response to the above questions, the student might be considering acute bronchitis and community-acquired pneumonia. The preceptor should now ask the student to identify the key features in the case that support both diagnostic considerations, including information in prototypical cases that might be missing in the present case.

Time constraints always exist in the ambulatory setting. To maximize student learning from this case, the preceptor should encourage the student to read independently. As described in chapter 1, this case represents an opportunity for the student to create an anchor prototype in memory for the typical presentation and course of community-acquired pneumonia. The student should read about the primary diagnosis and one other plausible explanation, using a compare-and-contrast strategy (5). This provides the student the opportunity to learn and remember features of competing diagnostic hypotheses that discriminate between the conditions under consideration. The preceptor can then follow up with the student on what was learned.

❖ Vignette 3: Priorities on Teaching Rounds

An experienced ward attending is pleased to have made the recent transition from paper-based charting to an electronic health record. After experimenting with several approaches to getting the work of patient care done efficiently so as to reserve time for a daily teaching session with the medical students, the attending settles on reviewing all chart notes and test results from home before rounds plus "real time" charting during rounds with the team.

Medical student: This patient is a 46-year-old woman we admitted yesterday with a 3-day history of cough, fever, and shortness of breath. She was in her usual state of health until...

Attending (interrupting): Okay, I read your admission history and know that you are considering pneumonia as your primary diagnosis. What did you find on lung exam this morning?

Medical student: She has decreased breath sounds on the right side and I think I hear some wheezing today that wasn't there yesterday.

Attending: Okay. I see she still has a fever with a maximum temp of 39.0°C at midnight last night. (Turning to the resident) Do you think she is better or worse today?

Resident: She's worse. Her respiratory rate is up to....

Attending (interrupting): Yes, I saw that. Let's go see her.

Attending (at the bedside, mobile computer at hand): *Hello, I'm Dr. Jones. How are you feeling today? Could I listen to your lungs?*

The educational challenge in this case, whether or not the attending realizes it, is to preserve meaningful participation for medical students and residents during inpatient teaching rounds when attending physicians face multiple competing agendas of quality patient care, efficiency, productivity, and clinical teaching (6). The introduction of electronic health records with remote access to clinical information has changed many aspects of patient care in teaching hospitals (7). This, coupled with time and productivity pressure, has added new challenges to team function.

The major difficulty in this scenario is a conflict in values that are desirable but incompatible: efficiency and time for learner development. Value conflict, even if both values are desirable, is a signal that a social theoretical approach may be most useful. From a social theory perspective, the preceding team interaction illustrates a teaching team trying to function with unclear rules and norms for integrating meaningful teaching into caring for patients. In this case, what the team must negotiate are roles, identities, structures, and resources so that both values can be maximized, but perhaps at different times. At least three scenarios are possible. First, when the team is on call and the values of efficiency and learning are equal, the team might explicitly negotiate the following roles: The senior resident manages the team, varying the approach and time spent teaching based on workload; the intern manages crosscover and new admissions; students learn their patients' stories and prepare concise, relevant presentations with guidance from the resident or intern; and the attending monitors from home and adjusts arrival time, informational needs, and teaching approach based on workload and team skills.

Second, when the team is post-call, the value of efficiency will trump learning because of work hour rules, thereby changing team members' roles. For example, the resident and attending briefly huddle to determine which patients need to be seen first by the team for patient care or educational issues. The intern and students present concise, relevant patient summaries that assume the attending has read the admission history and physical examination. The resident provides rationales for treatment decisions. The attending asks questions to elicit team members' understanding, adjusts teaching to address relevant gaps, and reviews important clinical findings at the bedside.

Third, on other days of the call cycle for a ward team, the value of learning will trump efficiency. Many different approaches are possible (Box 2-1). Attendings will need to consider the local design of the inpatient rotation. Because of information technology and time constraints, the attending can feel tremendous pressure to take over patient management. The preceding vignette shows that it is important to remember to avoid interruptions, clarify expectations for student and intern presentations during post-call rounds, and acknowledge the competing values at work. Social learning theory underscores the reciprocal nature of the environment and the community's (and individual's) behavior; each affects the other. Social theories also remind us that the participants are the custodians of the community's values. There always will be tensions. But education needs to remain central to the functioning of the ward team. And no one member of that community is more responsible for maintaining the centrality of the educational mission than the attending.

❖ Vignette 4: Student Transition to Clinical Learning

An experienced attending on the inpatient service arrives for a 2-week rotation with a team of two medical students, two interns, and a resident who have been working together for 2 weeks on the medicine wards. She decides to check in with the students.

Attending: How's it going?

Medical student 1: Pretty well.

Medical student 2: Actually, I'm frustrated. I heard that the medicine clerkship was the hardest but the best because of all the

---

Box 2-1. Approaches to Enhance Learner Development

- ▶ More extensive bedside teaching
- ▶ Separate time set aside for learners at the different levels to meet specific needs
- ▶ In-depth discussion of particular patient cases, including a review of the pathophysiology and critical appraisal of the clinical evidence for diagnostic and management decisions

teaching. But, that hasn't been happening on this team. The residents are so busy with all these patients that we never get any teaching. I want to go into medicine and I haven't gotten any feedback about how I'm doing. I'm starting to worry about my grade.

Medical student 1: *I agree. I wasn't going to say anything because I don't want to be a complainer, but I have no idea how I'm doing and I don't think I'm learning anything.*

Assuming that the students are, indeed, receiving a rich and varied clinical experience, including participating as active members of the ward team, the teaching challenge in this case then is to help the students' transition from learning in the classroom to learning from patient care (8). The third-year students are complaining of not getting enough teaching or feedback, primarily because they are used to experiencing teaching in a classroom or lecture setting and receiving behavioral feedback on tests. The "rules" have changed, and they don't "see" the teaching and learning to be gained from patients unless the resident or attending takes them to the whiteboard. The attending needs to create a more reflective approach to learning so that the students gain a sense of accomplishment as they work in the context of a busy clinical service. An experiential theoretical perspective, therefore, is appropriate.

From an experiential learning perspective, it is important to orient students to the nature of clinical learning through experience. Taking direct care of patients or participating in the care of others' patients is a *concrete experience*. Discussion of these cases is a form of *active reflection*. To the extent that general concepts and approaches to clinical cases are identified, the discussion also serves as *abstract conceptualization*. Students can then be encouraged to apply their learning to their patients, an example of *active experimentation*. It may help to be explicit about the fact that, in the past, someone else told the students what they needed to learn but now they are responsible for figuring out what they need to learn on their own. Asking students to identify learning goals for the rotation can facilitate this transition.

In this frame, the chaotic nature of a busy clinical service often interferes with active reflection. Students may fail to appreciate what they have learned and how to take this learning to the next clinical situation. It follows, then, that making time for the medical students is critical. The attending physician can negotiate with the supervising residents about who, how, and when this will occur. Opportunities for reflection include one-on-one discussion of individual patient care experiences, group case-based teaching separate from teaching or work rounds, and others depending on the structure of the training program.

❖ Vignette 5: Failure to Appreciate Illness Severity

It is October, and the intern is called to evaluate a patient on another service who is reporting shakes and chills. The patient was admitted 4 days earlier with ascites from chronic hepatitis C. The intern reviews the following chart note from this morning:

> **S:** *Hospital day 3 for hepatitis C/cirrhosis/ascites. Breathing easier. No new complaints.*
>
> **O:** *Tm 98.0, P 70-80, BP 125-135/70-85, R 12, Wt 103Kg (down 1.1)*
>
> **Sclera:** *Icteric*
>
> **Lungs:** *Clear*
>
> **CVR:** *Regular, no murmurs or gallops*
>
> **Abd:** *Distended, soft, nontender*
>
> **Ext:** *2+ edema to knees*
>
> **A/P:**
>
> *1. Hepatitis C/cirrhosis/ascites:*
>
> *- Continue diuresis w/goal 1-2 L out/day. Follow creatinine*
>
> *- Continue SBP prophylaxis w/cipro q wk*

The intern interviews and examines the patient who is alert, oriented, in moderate distress from a distended abdomen, but otherwise offers no complaints other than being cold. On examination, temperature is 98.9°F, pulse is 98 beats/min, blood pressure is 106/64 mm Hg, and respirations are 16 breaths/min. The intern notes scleral icterus, a dry mouth, normal jugular venous pressure, clear lungs, a regular heart rhythm without murmurs, a distended abdomen that is minimally tender diffusely, and 2+ pitting edema to the knees. This examination appears to be unchanged from earlier in the day. He concludes that the patient is cold and asks the nurses to get the patient more blankets.

The problem the teacher must address in this case is a missed diagnosis, or, more specifically, failing to appreciate how ill this patient really is. The intern has failed to recognize the patient's deteriorating vital signs and misinterprets the patient's symptoms (9). Assuming, of course, that the intern understands the importance of prompt diagnosis for a clinical situation as serious as this one, the learner difficulty appears to be insufficient experience with clinical situations like sepsis in patients with underlying medical conditions, so an experiential theoretical perspective is indicated.

One of the challenges for early interns is learning to function more independently in a setting of accumulating clinical experience while still being able to recognize one's own limitations. In this case, the intern probably has not had enough experience detecting more subtle clues in patients whose clinical situation is evolving. The residents and attending have a real role to play here, not only in being available to help evaluate ill patients but also to facilitate the interns' learning from experience (10).

From an experiential learning perspective, the resident and attending have the opportunity to engage the intern in reflection-on-action. As interns evaluate more and more patients independently, they are likely to make some errors. These errors are some of the most powerful opportunities for learning but require sensitivity in creating a learning climate that engages the interns in learning from their mistakes. The intern's concrete experience provides an opportunity for active reflection.

One powerful way to begin this discussion is to disclose a personal story of a mistake and the reflective learning that resulted from it. If appropriate, the moral of the story can demonstrate that teamwork can provide the checks and balances that help avoid these types of errors. For example, the attending could say, "I remember one time I evaluated a man on cross-cover for somnolence. I thought he was just 'sun downing.' Just as I was leaving, I thought to ask the nurse taking care of the patient what she thought. She mentioned that she was worried that, although normal, his blood pressure was dropping and his pulse rising—a sure sign of impending sepsis. I looked closer and, sure enough, he had hospital-acquired pneumonia." Reflection-in-action, or as in this case "after the action," enables learners to understand their clinical encounters and actions in ways that will be useful when similar cases are encountered in the future.

❖ Vignette 6: An Evolving Clinical Syndrome

Following a night on call, the intern is debriefing with the attending about a patient who had been transferred to the intensive care unit just an hour ago. The attending notices that the intern is visibly distressed.

> ***Intern:*** *We transferred Mr. Smith to the MICU because he dropped his blood pressure to 80/40 mm Hg. He's the patient we admitted yesterday with acute coronary syndrome. The nurse first called me when she noticed that Mr. Smith looked more anxious than he did an hour earlier. He was complaining of back pain and couldn't*

find a comfortable position in bed. His telemetry rhythm had been normal except for some premature ventricular contractions. When I reviewed his vital signs, I noticed that his pulse rate had been rising gradually over the previous 2 hours, although never exceeded 70. We doubled his metoprolol on admission, so I thought this trend might be important. Then he just crashed. We called the rapid response team. I'm really worried I missed something important.

Attending: *Let's make sure to save some time after attending rounds to follow up on Mr. Smith. I'm sure we'll be able to learn something.*

The teaching challenge in this case is to turn the intern's distress into a positive learning experience (11). Because it may be a knowledge or judgment problem, a cognitive theory perspective is appropriate. This scenario presents an opportunity to provide cognitive feedback.

The attending should start by asking the intern to summarize the patient's presentation on admission and the events of the night, including asking the intern for the initial problem representation. Then, ask the *team*, "Did we expect this outcome?" The goal is to compare the actual clinical outcome with the early diagnostic hypotheses and management decisions as a shared endeavor. If the diagnosis was missed, the attending should attempt to identify specific misunderstandings or key clinical clues that might have been overlooked. Ask for a formulation of a new problem representation that incorporates the back pain and deteriorating vital signs. The discussion should aim to explore and correct any partial understandings. The attending might ask, "Has anyone seen a case like this before?" followed by "Tell me about that case. How was it similar to or different from this case?" This line of questioning activates prior knowledge, building upon previously learned concepts or stored illness scripts. Next, invite the intern to explore the differential diagnosis for the new problem representation, including "must-not-miss" diagnoses.

Often, early learners will make predictable mistakes, and experienced clinical teachers can prepare teaching sessions designed to probe for such errors and capitalize on them in making teaching points. Learning from mistakes is more powerful than learning when everything goes well. In this case, the team missed a dissecting aortic aneurysm, providing the opportunity to explore assessment of back pain in the setting of acute coronary syndrome.

Finally, the attending should recommend a reading strategy that will help team members build strong knowledge structures and maximize learning from this experience. The intern should read about both the initial diagnosis of acute coronary syndrome and the subsequent diagnosis, dissecting aortic aneurysm, comparing and contrasting presentations, physical examination findings, and diagnostic testing approaches and results (5, 12).

By focusing on the complexities of the case and the patient's evolving signs and symptoms, cognitive feedback provides an opportunity not only to dissipate the intern's sense of failure, which clearly is an important outcome, but also to enrich his stores of illness scripts so that the lessons from this case will be accessible in the future.

❖ Vignette 7: Team Management Trouble

It is July and the beginning of an attending month on the medicine inpatient service. The resident is new to the team-supervising role. The medical students on the team seem rather sullen, and the interns are overheard complaining about their workload. On rounds, the resident interrupts the student during the case presentation.

> **Student:** *Our next patient is an older man who got up in the middle of the night and fell on his way to the bathroom. He did not lose consciousness, but thinks he almost passed out. He doesn't take any medications that…*

> **Resident (interrupting):** *His medications include metoprolol and HCTZ for hypertension so we were concerned about bradycardia, hypokalemia, or perhaps both.*

> *(One of the interns shows up a few minutes late for rounds and has not prerounded.)*

> **Attending:** *Okay, so is everyone here now? It seems like we're off to a bit of a rocky start.*

Assuming no extraneous issues, the teaching challenge in this case may be to help the new supervising resident establish a team management strategy that will address everyone's needs (13). From a behavioral theory perspective, orientation sessions at the beginning of new rotations provide the opportunity to clarify expected behaviors and consequences.

Failure to clarify expectations often leaves learners anxious and uncertain. Teachers—both attending physicians and supervising residents—should take the time upfront to clarify expectations with team members. It is possible that the new resident did not provide an orientation with clear, explicit, observable expectations for the interns and students. As supervisors of inpatient teams, residents must pay attention to their leadership roles and responsibilities. July is typically a particularly challenging period for managing this role. Interns are new to the role of doctor and both excited and fearful. Students may also be new to the role of clinical clerk. Stating expectations explicitly will lay the groundwork for smoother team function.

The attending should spend some time *alone* with the resident, checking in. Did the resident provide an orientation to relay expectations? If not, then a review of typical contents of such an orientation can be instructive. Orientation should address issues of professionalism such as punctuality, dress code, confidentiality, bedside manners, and timeliness of record keeping. In addition, the residents will want to establish ground rules for how the service will run, including who evaluates the patients in what order, when students will be observed, who presents cases on rounds and what type of presentation is expected, and when interns and students will be expected to ask for help or report patient status changes to the resident or attending. Finally, since evaluation and feedback are often associated with anxiety, clarifying how evaluation and feedback will occur is extremely important. If the resident did provide an orientation, then examining whether it was concrete and specific enough can be helpful.

❖ Vignette 8: Making Time to Teach

A second-year resident has just viewed her teaching evaluations from her last ward month as a supervising resident. Disturbed by what she finds, the resident seeks advice from the attending from that month.

> **Resident:** *Can I talk with you about our time together on the medicine wards in July?*

> **Attending:** *Sure. What's up?*

> **Resident:** *I just read my evaluations from the students and they are not very positive. The students criticized me for not including them in the management decisions on their patients. They really felt superfluous. I don't know what to do differently.*

The teaching challenge in this case is to help the resident new to the teaching role to develop teaching methods that provide medical students with meaningful participation. Since she has already started reflecting on the prior experience, an experiential learning perspective is most appropriate.

The resident's *concrete experience* leading her team and teaching medical students provides the opportunity for *reflective observation* and deeper learning. The attending should start with asking questions that facilitate recall of the experience, such as, "Tell me more about your approach to teaching the students on our team." This approach helps the attending to assess the resident's insight and potential readiness for change. The resident may confess that she is overwhelmed with clinical care responsibilities and unable to pay attention to the needs of the other team members. Or the resident may be oblivious to the social cues that things are not going well for the medical students. In either case, sharing observations, providing positive feedback, and eliciting the resident's reflective observations can facilitate the experiential learning process. For example, "I recall very clearly your efforts to include the students on teaching rounds. I liked your enthusiasm and efforts to stay positive given the workload the team was facing. Under time pressure, it is much more efficient to tell the students what to do for their patients rather than elicit their input. Do you think that was the situation?" This may trigger further reflections on the part of the resident. It will be important to facilitate the process of *abstract conceptualization,* providing the resident with a framework for teaching students and a conceptual approach to creating respectful, meaningful participation for less experienced learners while managing time (2). For example, the attending can suggest that the resident spend more time asking questions of the students rather than telling them what to do.

This serves three purposes. First, questions allow the resident to assess the students' knowledge and understanding of their patients' problems. Second, the students' responses will help the resident to focus her teaching points on the students' misunderstandings. Third, asking students for their input shows respect for them and creates meaningful participation, facilitating learning.

Guide the resident in *active experimentation* with a new approach to teaching students. In some cases the attending may need to model the approach for the resident, inviting her to watch the attending teach the students. In most cases, the resident will simply need to identify specific useful questions to accomplish the above approach the next time she is assigned to a ward rotation. Another ward month will provide the next *concrete experience* for the resident in learning to create meaningful participation for students.

❖ Vignette 9: Overlooked Complexity

On the medicine inpatient service in July, the attending observes the resident discussing one of the new patients on rounds. She is confident and enthusiastic. However, as the case unfolds, she appears to have overlooked several points of complexity in the case.

> **Resident:** *The patient was admitted last night after an episode of syncope. He's a 51-year-old man with multiple risk factors for coronary artery disease. Although he has no history of angina, when we questioned him further, he admits to experiencing substernal pressure when he mows the lawn. His exam was notable for a 2/6 murmur at the base, radiating up to his carotids. We put him on the rule-out MI protocol. His troponins have been normal and his ECG does not show any ischemia. He's feeling fine this morning and I think he's ready to go home and have an outpatient workup for CAD.*

The problem the attending must address in this case is the resident's failure to recognize clinical uncertainty. A cognitive learning perspective may be helpful.

As new supervisors of inpatient teams, residents must exercise judgment about what they can handle on their own and what requires input from others. Complex cases require attention to evolving, unfolding clinical syndromes, and avoidance of premature closure. The resident probably has developed nonanalytic thinking for common problems, but must be on the lookout for new signs and symptoms that would challenge conclusions drawn from pattern recognition. In essence, the resident must learn to "slow down" (14).

From a cognitive learning perspective, the attending physician should explore the resident's understanding of the case. Not infrequently in time-pressured situations, residents will present clinical cases and jump to the management plan, leaving the attending physician to infer the assessment or diagnosis. When this happens for complex clinical syndromes with ambiguity, stop the resident and ask for a one-sentence summary (the problem representation) in abstract terms. This step defines the clinical problem. Once there's agreement on the clinical problem needing to be solved, the attending should probe for understanding—"What is the plausible differential diagnosis for this case?" then "What is the most likely etiology?" then "What do we need to be sure we don't miss here?" then "How does your proposed plan for the day address these possibilities?" It is important to help the resident recognize 1) when the assessment step has been brushed over, 2) when the clinical case has unexplained elements that, when ignored, may lead to an incorrect diagnosis or plan, and 3) for complex clinical syndromes, how to build in a habit of asking "What else could this be?" or "Could I be wrong here?" or "What am I not seeing that I should be seeing"? or "What is missing?" or "What is puzzling me?" Such habits probably prevent premature closure and foster lifelong learning. By encouraging a watchful eye for subtle or nuanced features in clinical presentations, learners will build memory structures rich with case examples that extend beyond the prototypical case. To reinforce learning from each clinical case, the attending can review with the resident the answers to one of the aforementioned questions, probing for understanding.

❖ Vignette 10: Delinquent Charting

A second-year resident is having difficulty adjusting to the increased workload expected of him in continuity clinic. Although he enjoys evaluating new patients, has developed excellent relationships with patients on his continuity panel, and provides high-quality care, his preceptor notes that he is the last resident to finish his work week after week.

The practice medical director forwards the latest clinic performance report showing that this resident has 10 times more delinquent chart notes than any other resident in the practice. Attached is a handwritten comment, "You know we can't bill the patient's insurance company until the note is completed and signed electronically. This has got to change." The clinic nurse now forwards the following note: "Mr. Johnson called in asking if he should change his potassium. He was seen by (this resident) in clinic last week, and his diuretic dose was changed, but there is no note so I don't know if it was increased or decreased and what he intended to do about the potassium."

The problem the teacher must address in this situation is to help the resident see the relationships between delinquent charting, and both the potential medical error that could result and the functioning of the team. The resident is delinquent in charting, but it is not known whether this is due to a lack of time management skills or a lack of concern about the importance of timeliness. To best assist this resident, the preceptor will need to make this determination first. Spend some time *alone* with the resident, checking in. Is the resident aware that he is an outlier with regards to charting, and how does he react to this information? Does he seem contrite, frustrated, and overwhelmed—a sign that skill is the problem? Or, is he dismissive and unconcerned—a sign that attitude is the issue?

Time management is a skill. It can be completely defined and evaluated using objective measures, so if this is, indeed, a time management problem, a behavioral approach is appropriate. Remember that the resident needs to visualize good performance and then practice the skill with appropriate feedback. First, communicate the behavioral expectation and the reasoning behind it. Then, assist the resident with illustrations of appropriate performance. For example, the preceptor might say,

Preceptor: The expectation in this clinic is that residents get their notes done within 2 days of the visit. This is primarily a safety issue and a courtesy to colleagues who may need this information to care for your patients. I have noticed that your notes are very long and detailed. Take a look at this de-identified example of a note that is adequate and may be much quicker for you to generate. You might also want to review some of your own notes, looking for opportunities to create your own electronic templates for phrases you use commonly. You know, I have found it helpful to leave the clinic after I'm done with patient care and find a quiet place in the back office to complete my notes without interruptions.

While a behavioral approach provides information and external motivation, the goal is for residents to internalize the expectation of timeliness for themselves. If attitude is the issue and the resident does not believe timeliness is important, then a social learning perspective is useful. Social learning theory focuses on relationships, interactions, and values, much of which is best communicated by role modeling. How well do faculty members communicate the attitude that is a key component of patient safety?

Approaching attitude problems can be a threat to residents' self-esteem. It is important initially to suspend judgment about the *cause* or *appropriateness* of the attitude and focus on establishing a safe learning climate where the goal is improved performance. Identifying and then gently perturbing assumptions and beliefs is one useful approach (15). For example:

Preceptor: I know it can seem like we have nothing but rules around here. Why do you think we set such stringent requirements about getting the notes in?

Resident: I'm sure it has to do with JCAHO requirements and billing, and frankly I'm too busy to worry about that.

Preceptor: That's what the clinic managers would worry about, but it is really a professionalism issue—primarily patient safety and a courtesy to colleagues who may need this information to help care for your patients. Did you know that Mr. Johnson called yesterday about his potassium dose and we had to make a guess about what you had done with his furosemide? If we guessed wrong, he might end up with an arrhythmia due to hypo- or hyperkalemia. Could you check on what we did and make sure it was appropriate?

For attitudinal problems that recur, or occur across groups, rather than within individuals, it can be useful to create proactive exercises to help residents internalize appropriate values. For instance, overdue discharge summaries are a chronic problem for many training programs. To deal with this, one program developed an exercise as part of the residents' orientation. First, the program director led a discussion about the difference between a trade and a profession, noting that a profession contains a large body of specialized knowledge *and* polices its own standards. The residents then received real vignettes in which patient safety was compromised because of the lack of a discharge summary. The program director left the room so that residents and the chief resident could discuss the cases and establish their own proposed policies for delinquent discharge summaries. When the program director returned, the chief resident provided a blinded summary of the discussion and the proposed consequence—that residents not be allowed to rotate onto electives if there were any undicated charts for which they were responsible

This example illustrates residents accepting responsibility for policing themselves and a program granting them authority to determine the consequences if the self-determined expectations are not met, an approach supported by social learning theory.

❖ Vignette 11: Decision-Making Within a Hospital System

A second-year resident is presenting a patient undergoing preoperative consultation to the medicine consultation attending. The patient is scheduled for an elective hernia repair that same week. The surgical attending who referred the patient is known to be an outspoken opponent of the new hospital requirement for consultations on patients over 65 years of age undergoing general anesthesia.

> **Resident:** *So this patient is very healthy. He takes only aspirin and I told him to stop it 7 days before the surgery. He has never had lung or heart disease to his knowledge. On examination, his vitals are normal. Lungs are clear and he is moving air well. He has a grade III/VI crescendo/decrescendo murmur near the sternum that radiates to the neck and apex. He has paradoxical splitting of S2. His chest x-ray is clear and his cardiogram shows normal sinus rhythm and LVH by voltage criteria. He seems like he would be low risk.*
>
> **Attending:** *What do you make of that murmur and EKG?*

Resident: *Well the surgeon noted those in clinic last week too and didn't seem to be worried about them. I believe the case already is scheduled.*

Attending: *We may want to consider further workup.*

The teaching challenge in this situation is to assist the resident in identifying and addressing the hierarchical conflict that may be interfering with decision-making. The patient in the case as presented has a reasonable chance of having significant aortic stenosis, which would be a high-risk lesion that would preclude elective surgery until the valve was repaired. It is not clear whether the resident lacks this knowledge or is simply intimidated by the surgeon—in other words, whether the problem is a cognitive issue or a social one. To differentiate, the attending can change the context to remove the social intimidation and further probe the knowledge base. For example, the attending might say, "Suppose we have 2 months until the surgery. What, if anything, would you do about that murmur now?" If the resident recommends an echocardiogram to assess the possibility of critical aortic stenosis, then the teaching point now involves roles and power, and a social theoretical approach is appropriate. If not, the teaching point involves knowledge, and a cognitive theoretical approach is indicated.

From a cognitive theory perspective, the resident needs the opportunity to link this patient's examination to general knowledge about valvular heart disease and cardiac risk. Begin by engaging the resident in a discussion that probes the resident's current knowledge through a question such as, "What clinical problems are high-risk enough to warrant cancelling elective surgery?" It may become apparent that the resident is not familiar with general preoperative risk recommendations; the medicine consultation attending can then recommend reading any one of many guidelines or risk assessment schemes. On the other hand, the resident may understand that aortic stenosis is risky but be unsure whether this is aortic stenosis. Directing the resident to a physical examination text and audio recordings of typical systolic murmurs to compare and contrast aortic stenosis with another common systolic murmur, mitral regurgitation, would be appropriate. In either case, the assignment should include a specific time when the reading and listening will be reviewed and discussed. Alternatively, this may be an excellent opportunity to compare and contrast using bedside teaching of the cardiac clinical examination and special maneuvers.

If the difficulty is with roles and power, a social learning theory perspective may be most useful. In this vignette, there is a potential for hierarchical conflicts. For a resident, recommending cancelling surgery until the murmur can be properly evaluated is not easy, particularly when the surgeon is less than accommodating. Yet the resident needs to appreciate the proper priorities, or values, regardless of hierarchical concerns (16).

Recall that to make a social teaching point it is important to start with a shared value. In this vignette, the shared value is patient safety. The medicine consult attending can role-model the priority of patient safety while defusing the potential hierarchical conflict. This allows the resident to see how to frame the discussion from a patient safety standpoint. The attending can also offer to call the surgeon and provide support or role-model the discussion if the resident gets stuck.

❖ Vignette 12: The Busy Resident

The clinic nurse has been complaining loudly to one of the resident clinic preceptors today about a third-year resident.

> **Nurse:** *He always expects us to baby him. Last week he did a thoracocentesis and left a big mess of fluid-filled bottles and needles for us to clean up. His pancreatitis patient called for his monthly methadone. I paged him and he said, "Why don't you come to the ward and get the hard copy. I'm too busy to bring it to you." He asks us to do the HIV counseling even though it is hospital policy that the doctors must do it. The daughter of his dementia patient was here crying and stating that she wasn't able to care for him anymore. We called the resident and he just said, "Send her to the social worker."*

This resident demonstrates disrespectful behaviors with his clinical support team members, which threatens the teamwork required for patient care. The teaching challenge is to address this professionalism issue. Since the learner problem is consistent with either a behavioral or attitudinal problem, a behavioral or social learning theory perspective is indicated. The behavioral approach is concrete and quick, so it often is the default when there is time pressure. However, this approach does not allow for dialogue and establishment of shared goals, which are elements that may better help the learner to internalize collegial expectations.

A behavioral approach, if used, should identify the behavioral problem, the expected norm, the follow-up plan, and the consequences if not improved. For example,

> **Preceptor:** *Some of the clinic staff are frustrated with you. I need to hear your side of the story. They say that you are expecting them to clean up the mess after your procedures and to do some of your work, such as HIV counseling. Has this been happening?*

Assuming the resident admits to these behaviors, the preceptor can follow up:

Preceptor: In this clinic, we rely on teamwork and cooperation. The nurses are usually busy with triage and patient phone calls. When you leave the procedure tray for them to sort and dispose of properly, it takes them away from the tasks they do best to support you. You also need to know that hospital policy requires physicians do their own HIV counseling. I'd like for you to take responsibility for these things. Let's check back about this in 2 weeks to see how things are going.

From a social theory perspective, teaching begins with identifying a shared value. This may be the biggest challenge. For instance, if the proposed shared value is teamwork, it just may not be on the resident's radar, either because he is too busy or has been socialized to a different expectation of the doctor–nurse relationship. As always, social learning problems present an opportunity for reflection first. It is important initially to suspend judgment about the *cause* or *appropriateness* of the attitude and focus on establishing a safe learning climate where the goal is improving performance. Open-ended questions, immediacy, and self-disclosure may be helpful in these discussions. For example, the preceptor might start the conversation as follows, "What do you think your relationship with the nurses is like in this practice?" and then "If I were to ask the nurses, would they agree with you or describe it differently?" The preceptor may need to share the feedback from the nurses described earlier. It's hoped the resident will have some insight into his working relationships with his team members. The preceptor could then share a personal experience. For example, "I used to behave the same way. Then I realized that my phone triage was way worse than for my colleagues. So I talked with the nurses and learned what I was doing to undermine their work. It really made a difference for all of us to develop trust and respect. It's all about working together to take care of the patients. If any one of us shirks our part, it's harder for everyone else on the team."

As seen above, a social theory perspective is more involved but more likely to lead to real change and growth. A behavioral approach is used when you simply don't have time, or when other approaches have been tried, behavior is not changing, and clarity and fairness are desired before formal remediation.

❖ Summary

The teaching vignettes presented here are meant to represent some common challenges clinical teachers face and illustrate the link between learning theories and clinical teaching. Additional discussion of, and suggestions for, these very same challenges can be found in *Teaching in Your Office* (17) and *Teaching in the Hospital* (18), two other books in the *Teaching Medicine* series. The main point here is that once clinical teachers are able to identify the learner problem or teaching challenge and label it, the appropriate theoretical approach can be applied. The basic rule of thumb is this: If the issue is knowledge, use a cognitive approach; if the issue is skill, use a behavioral approach; if the issue is attitude, use a social approach. Not surprisingly, given the nature of clinical education experiential approaches cut across the domains of knowledge, skill, and attitude, particularly when learning problems call for reflection, with the goal being improved performance the next time around. Many clinical teaching situations are complex and may call for a combined approach. There is no one correct way to approach teaching challenges. However, the theories of learning presented here, particularly their applicability for specific teaching situations, should enable clinical teachers to better understand the challenges inherent in clinical education, expand their repertoire of teaching skills, and, ultimately, improve the patient care their learners provide now and in the future.

REFERENCES

1. **Pangaro L.** A new vocabulary and other innovations for improving descriptive in-training evaluations. Acad Med. 1999;74:1203-7.
2. **Skeff KM, Stratos GA, Berman J, Bergen MR.** Improving clinical teaching. Evaluation of a national dissemination program. Arch Intern Med. 1992;152:1156-61.
3. **Servis M, Smith S.** Diagnosing learner difficulties using a developmental framework for clinical teaching. Ann Behav Sci Med Ed. 2004;10:29-33.
4. **Chang RW, Bordage G, Connell KJ.** The importance of early problem representation during case presentations. Acad Med. 1998;73(10 suppl):S109-S111.
5. **Bordage G.** Elaborated knowledge: a key to successful diagnostic thinking. Acad Med. 1994;69:883-5.
6. **Irby DM.** What clinical teachers in medicine need to know. Acad Med. 1994;69:333-42.
7. **Peled JU, Sagher O, Morrow JB, Dobbie AE.** Do electronic health records help or hinder medical education? PLoS Med. 2009;6:e1000069.
8. **Chittenden EH, Henry D, Saxena V, Loeser H, O'Sullivan PS.** Transitional clerkship: an experiential course based on workplace learning theory. Acad Med. 2009;84:872-6.
9. **Bordage G.** Why did I miss the diagnosis? Some cognitive explanations and educational implications. Acad Med. 1999;74:S138-43.

10. **Westberg J, Jason H.** Fostering learners' reflection and self-assessment. Fam Med. 1994;26:278-82.
11. **Eva KW.** Diagnostic error in medical education: where wrongs can make rights. Adv Health Sci Educ Theory Pract. 2009;14 Suppl 1:71-81.
12. **Bowen JL.** Educational strategies to promote clinical diagnostic reasoning. N Engl J Med. 2006;355:2217-25.
13. **Wipf JE, Pinsky LE, Burke W.** Turning interns into senior residents: preparing residents for their teaching and leadership roles. Acad Med. 1995;70:591-6.
14. **Moulton CA, Regehr G, Mylopoulos M, MacRae HM.** Slowing down when you should: a new model of expert judgment. Acad Med. 2007;82:S109-16.
15. **Gazda GM, Childers WC, Walters RP.** Interpersonal Communication: A Handbook for Health Professionals. Rockville, MD: Aspen Publications; 1982.
16. **Pian-Smith MC, Simon R, Minehart RD, Podraza M, Rudolph J, Walzer T, et al.** Teaching residents the two-challenge rule: a simulation-based approach to improve education and patient safety. Simul Healthc. 2009;4:84-91.
17. **Alguire PC, DeWitt DE, Pinsky LE, Ferenchick GS.** Teaching in Your Office: A Guide to Instructing Medical Students and Residents. 2nd ed. Philadelphia: ACP Pr; 2008.
18. **Wiese J, ed.** Teaching in the Hospital. Philadelphia: ACP Pr; 2010.

3

Lessons for Teaching Effectively

Jay D. Orlander, MD, MPH

B. Graeme Fincke, MD

Teaching is a profession and a calling. Many doctors teach, but some do it more effectively than others. Each of us can visualize a particularly effective teacher, someone with whom we have had prior contact, extended or brief, who had a significant impact on our own professional development. Data from outside medicine suggest that teacher characteristics account for 30% of variance in student achievement (1). Similar data are not available for medical teaching, but experience suggests that teachers can make a substantial difference. Effective teachers inspire learners to become the best doctors they can be; sometimes they inspire us to be teachers ourselves. How do they do this? What makes teachers effective? What lessons do teachers need to learn?

While teaching may seem intuitive, effective teaching does not happen by chance. Good teachers work hard at it. Categorizing the practices of effective teachers into a few discrete groups has proven problematic (2, 3). Some authors lump or split these in varied ways: five dimensions and 16 attributes of great primary and secondary school teachers (1); eight characteristics of gifted university teachers (4); and six dimensions (5, 6), eight categories (7, 8), 12 qualities (9), 12 roles (10), eight skills (11), or 49 literature-derived themes of great clinical teachers in medicine (12). Upon closer inspection, however, these different schema send a consistent message.

KEY POINTS

- Successful teachers use a variety of teaching approaches, adjusting to the circumstances and needs of their learners' and the learning environment.
- Effective teachers engage with learners on an interpersonal level and, in the context of a trusting relationship, work with students to negotiate specific obtainable goals.
- Clinical teachers should observe trainees at the bedside, with patients, to formulate feedback based on first-hand data, as well as to create opportunities to demonstrate and role-model challenging clinical skills.
- Skilled teachers are well organized and prepared but must improvise regularly to maximize the experience for their students.
- Teachers who aspire to be most helpful to their learners become skilled in the art of teaching through a combination of reflection on their efforts, solicitation of feedback, and participation in organized faculty development activities.

This is not to say that effective teachers have identical personalities, or that they all excel in the same clearly defined clinical areas. They are all strong clinicians—that is a sine qua non for effective clinical teachers. But in addition, successful teachers exhibit similarities in affect and attitudes that set them apart. Effective teachers are knowledgeable; they enjoy and respect their learners; they are astutely aware of themselves, their environment, and their learners; and they use this information to alter their own behavior in real time to maximize the experience of the learner. They set goals such as engendering a desire for continued learning and exhibit a commitment to self-education, intellectual curiosity, and professionalism. The behaviors of the effective clinical teachers are driven by their awareness of the needs of the learner and modified by the clinical and environmental context of the moment. The most successful clinical teachers ally with their learners in the process of clinical care and bear witness to the behaviors of their students so that they can make direct observations and provide timely, specific feedback. There are technical skills in teaching that can enhance the efficiency of learning when used at the right time and in the right context. And effective teachers work at it: They find time to engage in self-improvement through faculty development workshops and through a process of self-discovery, self-awareness, and solicitation of feedback.

This chapter describes the most important lessons that can be learned from effective clinical teachers (Box 3-1). The lessons presented here are culled from examination of the literature, flavored by personal experience. As with many complex human processes, the lessons are not discrete—the concepts often overlap from one lesson to another.

❖ Lesson 1: Be Clinically Astute—and Wise

Knowledge and competence in clinical medicine are necessary to be a good clinical teacher. Without these, you lack credibility and, more important, abandon the learners to the stress of caring for patients at a time when they are not yet fully prepared. An important bulwark against this stress is the learners' confidence in the quality of guidance that they receive. Learners, particularly residents and fellows, highly regard extensive knowledge in their field as important. However, the depth and breath of knowledge needed to be considered knowledgeable by a clinical apprentice are somewhat context-dependent. Extensive knowledge is not synonymous with omniscience. Rather, what's needed is credible knowledge, to demonstrate the ability to care effectively for the most common cases and recurrent problems seen in one's practice environment. Clinical knowledge should reflect wisdom, judgment, and experience. The ability to expound on pathophysiology, cellular mechanisms, and genetic linkages may (or may not) be perceived as a plus to the learners, but such depth of knowledge is not necessary to being a successful clinical educator.

Box 3-1. Nine Lessons From Great Clinical Teachers

1. Be clinically astute—and wise
2. Fit teaching to learning
3. Be attuned to the learner and the environment
4. Engage learners and set goals
5. Observe and provide feedback
6. Demonstrate and role-model
7. Be organized and prepare
8. Improvise
9. To be effective, aspire to be great

More important, perhaps, than the amount of a teacher's knowledge is how that knowledge is imparted (see *Methods for Teaching Medicine,* another book in the *Teaching Medicine* series [13]). A teacher is most effective when the amount of information is "right sized," that is, adjusted for the learners' experience and modulated on the basis of the real-time context in which the learning is occurring. Experienced clinicians and effective teachers become facile in optimal management of common clinical situations, making decisions for diagnostic testing and in medical management almost unconsciously. They develop cognitive maps, or scripts (see *Teaching in the Hospital,* also part of the *Teaching Medicine* series [14]). These scripts enable effective teachers to express their thought processes deliberately, so that each step and its rationale can be clearly articulated for purposes of teaching. These teaching scripts assist in the efficient, often effortless, teaching to commonly seen cases.

Internal medicine requires an evidenced-based approach, yet the evidence increases hourly, the sources are seemingly infinite, and clinical decisions must be made in real time. The effective teacher knows what he knows and is comfortable putting forth the sources of the information, labeling ideas extracted from the literature versus those acquired by experience, and describing to the group where the sources of the clinical information intersect. The attending's capacity to say "I don't know" can generate the trainees' respect. The response of a teacher after the admission of ignorance often separates an effective teacher from a competent clinician who is less effective in the teaching role. A motivated student may volunteer or be given encouragement to find and report back with the answer. If the question is overly challenging, the teacher may seek the answer. In either case, accountability and commitment to shared learning are maintained.

❖ Lesson 2: Fit Teaching to Learning

There is no doubt that some gifted teachers exhibit exemplary behaviors, consistent with modern educational theory, because they have intuitively, or through personal trial and error, deduced that these are most effective. For many others inspired to improve their effectiveness as a clinical teacher, an understanding of teaching and learning theory can be very helpful (see also chapters 1 and 2 of this book). Insight into how information is learned, and the importance of self-motivation and relevance as a predictor of adult learners' educational achievement, will influence both how and what is taught. Since adults learn more when actively participating in discovery, the most effective teachers find ways to engage students in learning and allow them to take initiative in the educational process.

Rather than dictating dogma or answering directly, an effective teacher stimulates the learner to identify salient clinical questions and find her own answers. In medical school curricula, this principle manifests as fewer lectures and more problem-based (paper case-based) small-group learning. The clinical arena is the epitome of problem-based learning, so motivation is easily tapped into for those skilled in harnessing it.

A less effective educator may attempt to achieve this goal by simply handing all the students an article on hypertension and asking them to read it in the context of the first patient seen that month with this problem. In contrast, a more successful teacher will probe each individual student to appreciate what he or she knows about the assessment and treatment of the clinical problem (14), what decisions need to be made in caring for the patient at hand, and what else the student must know to make the best decision. By engaging the student in discussion, the teacher identifies the limits of the student's knowledge and helps lead the student toward a relevant question for that learner.

❖ Lesson 3: Be Attuned to the Learner and the Environment

Effective teachers help learners advance along their personal trajectory toward independent clinical competence or excellence. The best teachers are less interested in their own performance as teachers and more interested in the quality and quantity of learning that occurs. Students bring to their clinical assignments their own personal learning styles, personalities, life experience, and expertise. Because all these factors can influence learning, the best teachers get to know the learner and use this information to maximize the learner's experience. Being attuned to the learner means having an awareness of the student's past and present circumstances and the details of the systems in which they learn, and then using that information to influence one's own behavior to the maximal benefit of the student (Box 3-2). Effective teachers find out where the student is "at," the student's goals, and the problems the student is dealing with and modify their teaching to better fit with the student's circumstances.

Issues related to patient flow and systems of care (including idiosyncrasies in the admission or discharge procedures) affect the student's experiences. Effective teachers know the details of these processes, as well as the physical space and human and technological resources of the facilities at their disposal. For teachers to be effective, they must be familiar with relevant aspects of their trainees' educational program. Even after a review of formal orientation materials or proscribed goals from the clerkship or program directors, a chat with a learner can be very enlightening. For medical

Box 3-2. Being Attuned to Learners and Their Situations

1. Knowledge of learners
- ▶ Long- and short-term goals
- ▶ Relevant past clinical or life experience
- ▶ Level of clinical confidence and competence
- ▶ Degree and causes of stress or fatigue
- ▶ Learning style

2. Physical learning environment
- ▶ Characteristics of teaching space available
  - • Size of space relative to group size
  - • Physical comfort
- ▶ Cleanliness
- ▶ Temperature
- ▶ Noise
- ▶ Quality of furniture
- ▶ Lighting
- ▶ Technological resources available

3. Program considerations
- ▶ Program details
  - • Mandatory conferences/other program responsibilities for trainees
  - • Duration of rotation
  - • Program or clerkship director expectations
  - • Admitting rules/call schedule for inpatient rotations

4. Interpersonal learning environment
- ▶ Dyadic interactions or group dynamics
  - • How and where individuals arrange themselves
  - • How members interact

students, ascertaining what rotations have already been completed and how far along in their medicine clerkship the students are helps inform the teacher of the students' clinical exposure. For residents, asking about past rotations and understanding the on-call and clinic schedules and coverage responsibilities allow the teacher to anticipate barriers and take advantage of opportunities when planning teaching activities. Having this knowledge also enriches the bond between teacher and learner.

This bond is further enriched as teachers and learners come together as people. Teachers get to know and understand their trainees as people, both within and outside the medical context, including disparate social or political viewpoints, backgrounds, career goals, life experiences, and influences—any of these can affect a learner's motivation, perspective, or passion for clinical medicine. While such engagement (often mixed with some self-disclosure) helps to build a relationship between teacher and student, it also allows the teacher to understand how the learners think, where they can be motivated, and clinical situations to which they may be averse. Being informed of a student's life experiences, prior careers, or past research efforts also opens up potential resources for the teacher. Medical students may be prior pharmacists, lawyers, or psychologists. Some have spent many months studying a specific disease as part of a research team or dealing with a family member's chronic illness; others have expertise in medical ethics or health policy. These experiences are a resource that the attuned attending can use to enliven a discussion or provide a unique perspective during rounds. Effective teachers also are aware of the general state of learner confidence, clinical competence, and fund of knowledge. The level of confidence will affect behavior, such as willingness to speak in a group setting or demonstrate skills at the bedside. An assessment of trainee knowledge is critical in planning or engaging in teaching. Information targeted at too basic or too sophisticated a level for the audience will become a missed learning opportunity. Too basic, and the material will be considered redundant and probably boring. Too sophisticated, and it will be confusing. With no frame of reference, learners who lack the more basic knowledge cannot link the new information to anything and hence fail to build the proper mental framework. As a result, teaching that is not directed at the proper learner level is effort misused, inefficient, and irretrievable.

Emotion and fatigue modulate one's ability to be attentive to new information and affect the amount of learning possible. Mild to moderate stimulation is beneficial to effective learning, while extreme emotions, particularly negative ones, adversely affect student concentration. The gamut of emotion that affects students is wide. Situations outside the training environment (such as home life, family, and friends), although not directly associated with training, can affect it. Clinical work by its nature is unpredictable and potentially stressful. Sharing sadness with a patient suffering progressive or morbid conditions, losing confidence because a clinical diagnosis was off the mark or a case presentation went badly, feeling guilt when a patient interaction goes wrong or a clinical decision results in the deterioration of a patient's health—all of these will happen.

Fatigue is a common, if not chronic, state for many clinical trainees. Work and study hours combine to stretch many to their limits of endurance. While regulations are improving work hours, these limits will only mitigate what always has been and always will be a difficult and exhausting job. Despite the overall grueling nature, the work is frequently episodic in intensity. The number of patients cared for and the severity of their problems wax and wane by chance; some times are more challenging. Hence, whether in the clinic or the ward, there will be occasions when a learner is just worn out—too tired to pay attention, too tired to learn, maybe too tired to care. Effective teachers are attuned to what is going on with learners and use the information to modify their teaching. In this context, attunement implies a moment-to-moment awareness, which is essential to responding to the circumstances in real time.

Not all trainee emotions undermine the learning environment; some actually strengthen it. New clerks eager to learn internal medicine add energy to the clinic or hospital ward. After breaks from the clinical service for research blocks, vacation, or float responsibilities, house staff often return with renewed energy for primary clinical responsibilities as a basis for their learning. Creative teachers take advantage of such vigor to boost the learning expectations for themselves and the group.

Effective teachers also are conscious of the learning environment so that they have a chance of controlling it for purposes of improved education (15). The elements of the physical learning environment include the physical space, ambient noise, and temperature. Is the furniture comfortable, the lighting adequate, the temperature moderate? Are disruptions infrequent? If long discussions are held in a hallway and all parties are standing, how does that affect the quality and quantity of the discourse compared with encounters in a conference room, where parties are seated? How is the momentum for a discussion disrupted if the discussion is deferred until the parties can move to a room—how does that interruption differ if it takes just a minute or if the discussion must be delayed a lot longer? Effective teachers consider the tradeoffs and do their best to address these important environmental issues. So when a good teacher rearranges a few chairs, cleans a table, or moves a small group to conference space different from the one assigned, it may be out of consideration for comfort alone but is probably done to enhance the anticipated learning.

The style and tone of the interactions, as well as the manner in which people arrange themselves within a space, are also part of the learning environment. In a group of any size, one domineering, bombastic, or self-centered learner will stifle the interactions of others and detract from the learning of the group. Under such circumstances, an insightful teacher, who typically asks open-ended questions directed toward the group at large, may change styles and direct questions toward specific individuals to limit the influence of a single dominant participant. Awareness of the group dynamic while the attending is present or absent is relevant. Dyads that relate poorly or fractured team cohesiveness will negatively affect the way a group learns together. Attentiveness to interpersonal interactions will inform a good teacher's behaviors. Querying team members alone and identifying sources of angst early can diffuse the stress and allow for a better group experience.

❖ Lesson 4: Engage Learners and Set Goals

The clinical arena is chaotic in comparison to structured classroom or laboratory courses. Rotations are typically short, so that building relationships with the many different permanent staff members can be challenging, and peers (typically a source of support) working side by side are few at best. As a result, learners arriving on a new clinical rotation are often uncertain about their roles and responsibilities and are reasonably hesitant to fully engage with the personnel and the learning opportunities. The first task of a clinical teacher is to orient and engage with the learner in order to build an alliance focused on the learner's educational and professional development goals (14, 15). While the myriad tasks and information needed to successfully engage in clinical work can be overwhelming, learners and teachers alike benefit when they can come to an agreement on specific goals and objectives early in the rotation. The discussion should begin with student goals and expectations, and then should meld these with those of the teacher. In clinical medicine, some general goals are established by clerkship, residency, or fellowship program directors, but there is still benefit from explicit interpretation by the teacher and learners. It is common for goals to evolve over time, and renegotiation happens to a greater or lesser degree throughout a rotation. Good teachers set the bar high (3). They expect a commitment from the learner to his own education and provide a promise of reciprocity from themselves.

The approach used to engage a trainee takes different forms for the different stages of clinical learners. Medical clerks are anxious to delve into clinical care; hence, short periods of independence in which they are alone with patients to initiate interval histories allow them to test and try out their new skills. Independence must be balanced with observation and demonstration, but having a student shadow a more seasoned trainee or an attending full-time is not adequately engaging to them. The veteran teacher knows that fewer, more engaging patient encounters are more profitable to early learners than a whirlwind of cases flashing past them with little time to engage with patients or teacher. For more advanced trainees, such as senior residents or fellows, adequate engagement may mean pressing for assessments and plans in clinically challenging patients, sharing teaching responsibilities for interns or students, identifying a clinic-based practice improvement project, or pushing to review the newest literature relevant to a few selected cases. In these instances new, more challenging goals are negotiated that keep pace with the learners' professional development.

The ultimate goal in engaging learners is to foster self-motivated clinicians. In the early phases, good teachers stimulate learners in a way that encourages success by helping them to identify appropriate questions and, at times, leading them to proper places to find the answers. For less advanced trainees, assignments should not be too broad because an inexperienced student can get lost in the density or volume of information (for example, trying to learn everything about diabetes in one night) or too narrow, wherein information is too limited or too technical. The latter questions are best left to a more advanced trainee or the teacher—someone who has the perspective to present a balanced representation of limited or conflicting data. Therefore, adequate stimulation means steering students toward appropriate questions for their personal level of achievement.

❖ Lesson 5: Observe and Provide Feedback

Effective clinical teachers gather data on their trainees first-hand. They watch the trainees interact with patients, all the while collecting and processing data and providing direct patient care, education, and support. An attending's availability must not be limited to a conference room or office. Successful clinical teachers must be available to go to the patient's side. Where else can one validate a trainee's skill in communication and physical examination? On inpatient rotations, many differing interactions should be witnessed, such as peer to peer, resident to intern or student, trainee to nursing staff. Because clinicians must also be effective in working with consultants and allied health staff, clinical teachers should watch trainees interact with these personnel (14). Likewise, observing learners interact with patients in the office or at the bedside is efficient and should be the rule, not the exception (16).

In a clinical environment, the trainee behaviors that should be observed are numerous because they should be representative of all the skills to be mastered. Good teachers listen attentively to complete case presentations, through which they hear a student's decision-making process and problem-solving strategies. Reading chart notes and attending to types of questions learners ask gives the teacher more information about a learner's knowledge and thought process. These and other observations are the basis for feedback (Box 3-3).

Feedback follows clinical observation and can be considered information provided to improve future performance. This is formative information and contrasts with information that is summative (that is, end-of-rotation assessment of achievement). Feedback is most effective when given in the setting of an alliance between teacher and learner, wherein both parties

---

Box 3-3. Guidelines for Giving Feedback

1. Give feedback in the setting of an alliance between learner and teacher in which improving learner skills is an explicit expectation.
2. Base feedback on direct observations (notes taken during the encounter are a very helpful resource).
3. Make feedback timely (as close to the observation as possible) because this helps with recalling detail.
4. Start with learner self-assessment and reaction to improve diagnosis of the cause of any suboptimal behavior.
5. Use nonjudgmental language.
6. Be very specific (note sequence of events, verbal and nonverbal actions and reactions).
7. Focus on behaviors.
8. When discussing attitudes, label them as the observer's perception, an interpretation based on the specific actions of the trainee (behavior can only imply attitude).
9. Remember that validation of appropriate skill is also a form of feedback (this serves to solidify emerging skills).
10. Brainstorm suggestions for improvement.
11. Make sure feedback occurs frequently, is expected, and is solicited.

agree that the goal is to help the trainees improve their mastery. Skill in one domain should not be extrapolated from skills in a different domain, such as assessing physical examination skills only through oral case presentations. Any observed behavior related to professional development is appropriate for feedback, including tasks, processes, and behaviors. Of course, behaviors can suggest or imply attitudes, which also need to be addressed, but these should be labeled by teachers as their own perception.

Feedback discussions should begin with asking the learner to self-assess. Ideally, learners will be accurate; some may be overly self-critical. If performance was suboptimal, the teacher should try to identify the cause of the problem to better help the student identify a corrective plan. The language used in feedback discussions needs to be nonjudgmental, avoiding critique of character but staying focused on specifics of observed behavior. Feedback should include an action plan learners can pursue to bring them closer to their goals. Feedback should happen as close in time to the observation as is feasible and should recur with great frequency (17).

Observation and feedback require time; they also require being in the right place at the right time. This may necessitate moving beyond the corridor and scheduled conference room sessions. Being around more means being able to take advantage of the teachable moments that present themselves. Teachers must make time to listen to the trainees' concerns, field clinical questions, or review cases when necessary. Like college professors who stay after class to answer questions, hold office hours, and review sessions to help their students, so too should clinical teachers be available beyond the designated hours for rounding on new patients, leading attending rounds, or holding a preclinic conference. Writing notes in the same work area with the learners, lingering after attending rounds, and joining the team for a meal makes the teacher physically accessible to learners. This accessibility gives learners the opportunity to approach the teacher alone or in small groups to follow up on a concern. Being physically present does not always equate with being fully accessible to the learners. The learners need to know that they will get the attention they need, and that such requests are encouraged and met with enthusiasm. Glancing at the clock while asking if there are more questions sends a not-so-subliminal message that additional questions aren't welcome. Tone of voice, body language—all the nonverbal as well as verbal signals need to be sending the same message: I am here if you need me.

❖ Lesson 6: Demonstrate and Role-Model

Basketball coaches do not just talk to a youngster about how to shoot the ball; they take a ball onto the court, position their body, hands, and arms in the appropriate manner, and go through the motions of shooting the ball at the basket. All the while they may be explaining what they're doing and why, but the demonstration is equally as if not more important than the verbal description. Why should a medical coach be any different (14)? The best clinical teachers don't just tell their students what to do, they show them. This principle of demonstration applies not only to physical examination but across the spectrum of clinical skills required in the practice of medicine, from case presentations to history-taking, patient education, counseling, even the writing of notes and discharge summaries. If a student struggles in organizing data in a case presentation, a good teacher tells the student what she should do to improve. A better teacher takes the next step and demonstrates how to present the data. A still better teacher begins by asking the student where she is having difficulty. The demonstration is then a directed one, gauged to address the student's particular problem (or the student's misconception of the nature of the difficulty, once it has been brought to light). Demonstrations can occur through role-playing, on each other, or with real patients. Showing is the critical part (15).

Accompanying an intern to query a consultant or meet with a family and reviewing images with the radiologist alongside the resident are some of the clinical activities in which good teachers partake with a trainee so that they can observe and, if appropriate, demonstrate proper attitude, technique, or skill. This is particularly important when learners are uncertain or when the clinical stakes are high. At these times it is essential to be in the trenches with the learners. The learners will deeply appreciate this effort, and it will strengthen the bond between teacher and learner.

Considered in greater detail in *Mentoring in Academic Medicine*, another book in the *Teaching Medicine* series (18), it is crucial to appreciate that clinical teachers serve as role models in all aspects of their behavior. This may or may not always be desirable, but it is true. Interactions with patients, colleagues, nurses, allied health, and clinical support staff are all observed by trainees. Effective teachers take advantage of this and consciously perform for the audience they know is watching and learning. Conscious of their role model status, effective teachers often engage in a behavior for the sole purpose of demonstrating a technique or skill for the learners (19). Asking a probing follow-up question to a patient not only elicits useful clinical information but also demonstrates to the observers what information is important to obtain or how it should be obtained. Rather than explaining to a resident how to assess medication adherence, a good teacher who observes a trainee struggling with this skill may engage the patient directly and demonstrate how to make the assessment with the resident present.

The clinical arena provides numerous opportunities for role-modeling. The teacher can focus on history-taking, physical examination, or attitudes and behavior. Effective teachers are models not only of knowledge and skill but of attitudes that, once engendered, may accompany students throughout their professional lives. Patient-side presentations offer many occasions for the attending to intervene with history-taking techniques or demonstration of physical findings. Inevitably, a challenging communication task arises, such as delivering bad news or educating a patient about a new condition. A good teacher will use such a moment, take time to plan for the encounter with a trainee, and then negotiate to either role-model or observe the discussion.

It is helpful to alert the learners that a demonstration is about to take place so that the students attend to details of behavior or language they may otherwise not perceive and that can be explained in later discussion. Debriefing about the encounter afterward helps complete the educational loop. If the encounter was emotionally powerful, discussion of the impact on the patient or trainee is important in the process of professional development.

❖ Lesson 7: Be Organized and Prepare

Preparation is important for all teaching activities. Time management in a case conference is achieved by spending time before the session establishing a hierarchy of important teaching points for the case. Even when a common topic is being discussed for the 30th time, a few preparatory minutes allows the teacher to consider how to expand or contract the discussion in response to what he learns of the group's knowledge and interest in real time. Less seasoned teachers may need more planning time, but experience is never a substitute for planning. Good teachers are organized— they don't use the learners' time to organize themselves. Medicine is complicated, and diagrams, tables, or even calculations are sometimes useful in helping learners develop a deep understanding of a complex topic (for example, see the dialogues in *Teaching in the Hospital* [14]). Good teachers prepare these in advance. Drawing a diagram on the board before the learners arrive or distributing copies of a table respects the learners' time and allows a teaching session to flow without interruption.

Adequate preparation also includes selecting the right tool for the job. Too often, younger teachers equate preparation with a PowerPoint lecture. A copy of a relevant clinical guideline, a series of prepared questions, a road trip to the hematology laboratory, or a brainstorming session using just the white board as the primary teaching tool may make for active engagement of the learner and more optimal learning. Good teachers match the teaching tools to the teaching goals, the interests of the group, and their own skills and comfort with various approaches. There is no one best path, but rather a range of methods and roles from which to choose in order to maximize effectiveness.

Indeed, effective teachers often are "overprepared." Being overprepared means having the ability to alter the presentation on the basis of the needs and desires of the audience on the fly. The more prepared you are, the easier it is to improvise, that is, shift the direction of the presentation while remaining articulate and coherent. For example, a seminar leader, after opening a session with 20 minutes of prepared comments, might field questions from the audience. Having "overprepared," she can then select the most relevant material from what she is prepared to present, and tailor the presentation especially for her audience. "Overpreparation" may be a misnomer. In actuality, effective teachers consider several alternative directions a presentation could go and contemplate using different segments of information while adapting to the needs of the group in real time. A pitfall that less experienced teachers who meticulously prepare sometimes encounter is becoming wedded to the prepared structure. As a result, they feel less able to respond flexibly to what is happening in the moment. This can be called "tripping over the lesson plan," which is one way to become *less* effective. But when used properly, overpreparation increases flexibility and the capacity to improvise.

Organized teachers keep an eye on the clock. Required conferences, patients to see, notes to write, or books to study for upcoming exams are some of the competing activities for trainees' time that may be awaiting them after a teaching session. Once a teaching session encroaches on the next activity, most attendees' minds are already considering the next task and are not fully attentive to the teacher. Effective teachers monitor the time and know when and how to wrap a session up. Often a bit of improvisation is required. Well-prepared teachers do this well.

❖ Lesson 8: Improvise

The concept of improvisation has been woven into several of the lessons above but deserves additional attention. Improvisation can take several forms. First is an aptitude to perform without a fixed or rigid script, calling instead on one's personal store of knowledge, skill, and clear, quick thinking. This type of improvisation is described earlier, where a well-prepared seminar leader may improvise part of a presentation in response to the interests and knowledge of the audience. This also applies to discussions of new cases or consultations, wherein the learners can see the teacher organize and address problems in real time. Which teaching technique they choose is part of the improvisation: role-modeling, demonstration, Socratic discussion, mini-lectures, and so forth. The second form of improvisation is an ability to deviate from a prepared script when unanticipated circumstances arise. Effective clinical teachers are great improvisers. They use all of their know-how and then apply excellent judgment in determining when deviation from the initial plan is likely to improve the long-term goal. The ability to improvise is a desirable trait in many professions, actors, musicians, and quarterbacks, to cite a few. The improvised performance may be so expert as to seem preplanned. Successful improvisation requires that the central character be knowledgeable and attuned to the circumstances and other individuals with whom they are interacting. Examples of this type of improvisation include delaying teaching rounds to console a distraught patient or family, forgoing a planned talk on renal failure when a discussion of diabetic management better fits with the more pressing problem of the day, or canceling a talk completely to have an open discussion on dealing with end-of-life concerns when such an issue arises.

The final form of improvisation is balancing the competing demands on the clinical teacher: addressing the needs of patients as well as all individual learners (13). Balancing these priorities is a constant challenge. On inpatient rounds, for example, at least four demands are operating at any given time, and the teacher must choose the most appropriate: 1) ensuring that the patient gets the highest-quality care (patient supervision); 2) ascertaining and pursuing the aspects of the case that will promote learning (educational agenda); 3) monitoring the progress of discussion (group process); and 4) encouraging participation of individual learners (fostering student development). This is where the teacher must improvise, switching from one priority to another, sometimes dealing with multiple priorities at once, all in relation to shifting goals that relate to the different domains of responsibility.

❖ Lesson 9: To Be Effective, Aspire to Be Great

The final lesson speaks to the standards effective teachers bring to their work. To be effective, aspire to be great. Perhaps the single most important characteristic of effective teachers is that they try to be the best possible teachers they can be, to have their learners come away with something useful from each encounter. While good teaching may seem intuitive to some, high-level skill does not happen by chance. Those who desire to improve their teaching effectiveness do so by working hard at it and using many different strategies. Little has been said here about the specific skills required for teaching. These include how to select and ask questions, how to deliver a lecture, and how to run a workshop or discussion. The message here is not that these skills are unimportant. They are quite important, and are covered in detail throughout the *Teaching Medicine* series, particularly in *Methods for Teaching Medicine* (13). The message here is that these skills must be deployed creatively and driven by an unabiding commitment to the learners.

Few are born great teachers. Proficiency develops over time. Motivated by the fulfillment they receive from the task of teaching and an earnest desire to help learners, effective teachers work hard. They participate in faculty development programs (see chapter 4 of this book), building skills for different aspects of the job. Those who aspire to improve their teaching learn from failure and success, through solicitation of feedback, reflection, and practice (20, 21). Great teachers do not shy away from trying new approaches. Never letting perfection be the enemy of good, they apply and refine innovative ideas and clinical skills into new teaching tools. Teaching tools do not equate exclusively with technology but rather, with more personal strategies applied at the right time and in the right context.

❖ Conclusion: Applying the Lessons

Students are witnesses to what effective teachers do. But the story is more complex than analyzing specific behaviors. Effective teachers share an attitude that places learners and learning ahead of all else. They are successful because they find ways to partner with their students in pursuit of professional development.

Learning is all about personal discovery, and a good guide will allow a person's journey to go farther in the same amount of time by making it more efficient, by encouraging travel along the correct path, and by removing obstacles, both seen and unseen. An effective educational guide also makes the journey more fun by pointing out the key sights when they are there to be seen, even when camouflaged or subtle. The most important concept for new teachers to appreciate is that the relational aspects between them and their learners are as critical as the technical aspects of their teaching. So if you are motivated to become a more effective teacher, or better still a great teacher, work at it. Both you and your students will benefit enormously.

REFERENCES

1. **Hattie J.** Teachers make a difference: what is the research evidence? Paper presented at Australian Council for Educational Research, Distinguishing Expert Teachers from Novice and Experienced Teachers. October 2003. Accessed at www.acer.edu.au/documents/RC2003_Hattie_TeachersMakeADifference.pdf.
2. **Brookfield SD.** The Skillful Teacher. 2nd ed. San Francisco: Jossey-Bass; 2006.
3. **Bain K.** What the Best College Teachers Do. Cambridge, Massachusetts: Harvard Univ Pr; 2004.
4. **Mohanan KP.** Assessing quality of teaching in higher education. Centre for Development of Teaching & Learning. Accessed at www.cdtl.nus.edu.sg/publications/assess/who.htm.
5. **Irby DM.** Clinical teacher effectiveness in medicine. J Med Educ. 1978;53:808-15.
6. **Irby D, Rakestraw P.** Evaluating clinical teaching in medicine. J Med Educ. 1981;56: 181-6.
7. **Ramsey PG, Gillmore GM, Irby DM.** Evaluating clinical teaching in the medicine clerkship: relationship of instructor experience and training setting to ratings of teaching effectiveness. J Gen Intern Med. 1988;3:351-5.
8. **Ramsbottom-Lucier MT, Gillmore GM, Irby DM, Ramsey PG.** Evaluation of clinical teaching by general internal medicine faculty in outpatient and inpatient settings. Acad Med. 1994;69:152-4.
9. **Azer SA.** The qualities of a good teacher: how can they be acquired and sustained? J R Soc Med. 2005;98:67-9.
10. **Harden RM, Crosby J.** AMEE guide no 20: The good teacher is more than a lecturer—the twelve roles of the teacher. Medical Teacher. 2000;22:334-47.
11. **Ramani S, Leinster S.** AMEE guide no. 34: Teaching in the clinical environment. Medical Teacher. 2008;30:347-64.
12. **Sutkin G, Wagner E, Harris I, Schiffer R.** What makes a good clinical teacher in medicine? A review of the literature. Acad Med. 2008;83:452-66.
13. **Skeff KM, Stratos GA, eds.** Methods for Teaching Medicine. Philadelphia: ACP Pr; 2010.
14. **Wiese J, ed.** Teaching in the Hospital. Philadelphia: ACP Pr; 2010.
15. **Skeff KM, Stratos GA, Berman J, Bergen MR.** Improving clinical teaching. Evaluation of a national dissemination program. Arch Intern Med. 1992;152:1156-61.
16. **Alguire PC, DeWitt DE, Pinsky LE, Ferenchick GS.** Teaching in Your Office: A Guide to Instructing Medical Students and Residents. 2nd ed. Philadelphia: ACP Pr; 2008.
17. **Ende J.** Feedback in clinical medical education. JAMA. 1983;250:777-81.
18. **Humphrey H, ed.** Mentoring in Academic Medicine. Philadelphia: ACP Pr; 2010.
19. **Wright SM, Carrese JA.** Excellence in role modelling: insight and perspectives from the pros. CMAJ. 2002;167:638-43.
20. **Orlander JD, Gupta M, Fincke BG, Manning ME, Hershman W.** Co-teaching: a faculty development strategy. Med Educ. 2000;34:257-65.
21. **Pinsky LE, Irby DM.** "If at first you don't succeed": using failure to improve teaching. Acad Med. 1997;72:973-6; discussion 972.

4

Becoming a Better Teacher: From Intuition to Intent

Yvonne Steinert, PhD

Passion, hope, doubt, fear, exhilaration, weariness, colleagueship, loneliness, glorious defeats, hollow victories, and above all the certainties of
surprise and ambiguity ... How can one begin to capture the reality of
teaching in one single word or phrase? The truth is that teaching is frequently a glorious, messy pursuit in which surprise, shock and risk are
endemic... (1).

—Stephen D. Brookfield

The rewards of teaching have been identified at the beginning of
this book. So have theoretical frameworks for teaching, notions
of how competency is attained, and a description of what the
best teachers do. This chapter builds on these themes by examining
how teachers can become better at what they do.

However, we first need to understand what "better" means or,
more specifically, what defines the process of becoming a better
teacher. Many educators have addressed this question and suggested
that the process of becoming a better teacher refers to modifying
teaching behaviors and replacing ineffective teaching strategies and
techniques with more effective ones (2). For the purpose of this discussion, becoming "better" will refer to the process of becoming a
more effective teacher and *improving performance* in teaching.
Moreover, becoming a "better teacher" will include changes in teach-

KEY POINTS

- Becoming a better teacher is a complex process that includes both formal and informal approaches, in individual and group settings.
- Learning to teach from experience involves learning by doing, observing others, and peer and student feedback.
- Self-awareness, critical analysis, and the development of new perspectives are fundamental to reflective practice.
- Becoming a member of a teaching community and valuing learning in the work place is an important step in becoming a better teacher.
- Faculty development is a social practice that can take on many forms, including workshops, fellowships and longitudinal programs, and advanced degrees.
- Becoming a better teacher, which encompasses changes in teaching practices, beliefs, and attitudes, is grounded in pursuing your passion and the rewards of teaching.

ing practices, beliefs, and attitudes, with the goal of improved student learning.

What is required? First, we need to appreciate that becoming a better teacher is a *process*; one does not become a better teacher overnight. It is hard work. Moreover, the process generally starts with a desire to teach— and to improve. As an experienced teacher commented, "It starts with the notion of *wanting* to become a better teacher. Intrinsic motivation and volition are key. So is the need to nurture your interest and your passion" (3).

In addition, accurate self-assessment and a working knowledge of what constitutes effective teaching are key. What, then, are the core competencies of teaching? What techniques need to be mastered? What do the best teachers do?

With these questions before us, this chapter begins with a brief review of the core competencies for teaching and the pedagogic principles that guide better teaching. Next, this chapter describes how one can become a critically reflective teacher and an astute "student" of one's own performance. You need to know what is expected of you. What are the competencies that you need to master? What are the tasks at hand? Knowing what you need to accomplish—and in what time frame—can often help to initiate a process of self-improvement. Informal and formal approaches to faculty development are then discussed, including how to construct a personalized plan for faculty development. True to the cyclical nature of this or any process in which one tries, learns, and then tries again, this chapter concludes where it began, with a discussion of the joys of teaching, including the joys that come with a sense of getting better.

❖ Competencies and Pedagogical Principles

In chapter 3, Jay D. Orlander and B. Graeme Fincke identify many characteristics of the effective teacher. Earlier work on this same subject includes Irby's (4) report, which showed that students value the following characteristics in their teachers: enthusiasm, a positive attitude toward teaching, rapport with students and patients, availability and accessibility, clinical competence, and subject matter expertise. Several core teaching skills have also been identified. These include the establishment of a positive learning environment, the setting of clear objectives and expectations, the provision of timely and relevant information, the effective use of questioning and other instructional methods, appropriate role modeling, and the provision of constructive feedback and objective-based evaluations (5). Although many frameworks for defining teaching competencies are now available (5–7), it is helpful to choose one that resonates for you and to use it as a guide to self-assessment, personal development, and career planning.

Teachers often question their role. In an interesting article, Harden and Crosby (8) outline six areas of activity that guide the teacher's role: information provider, role model, facilitator, assessor, planner, and resource developer. As these authors state, each role demands both clinical content and educational expertise, and each requires different levels of contact with the learner. Hesketh and colleagues (6) built on this framework by defining the competencies of the "excellent" clinical teacher, which include *what* the physician is able to do (for example, teach large and small groups), *how* he or she approaches teaching (for example, with an understanding of principles of education and with appropriate attitudes), and the physician as a *professional* (for example, understanding his or her role in the organization; participating in professional development). Table 4-1, which summarizes these core competencies, can further facilitate self-appraisal.

Experienced clinical teachers usually have general conceptions of teaching and learning in addition to a repertoire of teaching strategies (4). That is, they usually possess knowledge of specific behaviors, strategies, and instructional techniques, but few understand the underlying theories, principles, and concepts of the teaching and learning process (9).

Table 4-1. Core Competencies for Teachers

Performance of tasks: technical intelligences ("doing the right thing")

What the doctor as a teacher is able to do:

1. Teach large and small groups
2. Teach in a clinical setting
3. Facilitate and manage learning
4. Plan learning
5. Develop and work with learning resources
6. Assess trainees
7. Evaluate courses and undertake research in education

Approach to tasks: intellectual, emotional, analytical, and creative intelligences ("doing the thing right")

How the doctor approaches teaching:

8. Intellectual intelligence: With understanding of principles of education (e.g., learning styles, distance learning, principles of change)
9. Emotional intelligence: With appropriate attitudes, ethical understanding, and legal awareness (e.g., enthusiasm, empathy and interest, respect)
10. Analytical and creative intelligence: With appropriate decision-making skills and best evidence-based education (e.g., prioritizes workload as teacher, uses evidence–based medical education as the basis of teaching)

Professionalism: personal intelligences ("the right person doing it")

11. The role of the teacher or trainer within the health service and the university (e.g., understands teaching responsibilities; maintains acceptable balance between service, teaching, and research)
12. Personal development with regard to teaching (e.g., reflects upon and is aware of own strengths and weaknesses; keeps abreast of new teaching and learning techniques)

Adapted with permission from Hesketh E, Bagnall G, Buckley E, Friedman M, Goodall E, Harden R, et al. A framework for developing excellence as a clinical educator. Med Educ. 2001;35:555-64.

Moreover, this knowledge is often considered "tacit," and few teachers can articulate their understanding of core knowledge and principles (10). In an interesting study, McLeod and colleagues (9) identified the important concepts and pedagogical principles, which, if known and understood by clinical teachers, could enhance their "teaching prowess and success." These concepts fall into four main categories: *curriculum,* which includes goals and objectives and curriculum structure and design; *how adults learn,* which encompasses motivation for learning, transfer and self-regulation of learning, and adult learning theory; *helping adults learn*, which incorporates pedagogical implications of learner differences, role modeling, and problem-solving for learning; and *assessment*, which consists of summative versus formative assessment, criterion versus norm referencing, and performance-based evaluation. Because there is also good reason to believe that knowledge of the principles of pedagogy can sensitize teachers to the process of teaching and learning, and can serve as a critical organizing function to effective practice, clinicians intent on becoming better teachers may well also want to explore these concepts in greater detail (9).

❖ Approaches to Becoming a Better Teacher

As Figure 4-1 illustrates, approaches to becoming a better teacher can be classified along two dimensions: informal versus formal learning and individual versus group contexts. At one end is the teacher who reflects on his or her attending rounds and decides (on his or her own) how things went and how they might have been done differently. This strategy is informal and individual, although (as will be described below) it can be enriched greatly by understanding *how* one can learn from experience, and by using tools to aid that process. At another end is the teacher who enrolls in a formal program for faculty development and works alongside colleagues, following a curriculum designed to address specific learning needs. This is a formal, group-based approach, but as will be discussed, it will be more effective if the course and curriculum are selected deliberately, on the basis

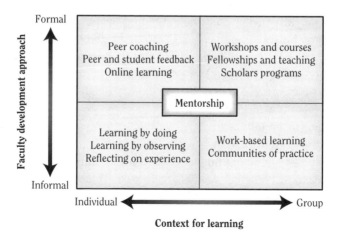

Figure 4-1 On becoming a better teacher.

of explicit criteria. Nested in the center of Figure 4-1 is mentorship. This is intentional because any strategy for becoming a better teacher benefits from the support and challenge that an effective mentor can provide.

❖ Learning (to Teach) From Experience: Doing, Observing, Using Feedback

Clinical teachers often acknowledge that they became adept at what they do by "the nature of their job responsibilities" and "learning on the spot" (3). This is an excellent example of experiential learning—whether the teaching occurs in the classroom or in the clinic, in an outpatient or an inpatient setting. Learning (to teach) from experience can be divided further into three categories: learning by doing, learning by observing, and learning from peer and student feedback. Learning from reflection is discussed in the next section.

Learning by Doing
The learning cycle is described by Kolb and Fry (11) and is presented in greater detail in chapter 1 (see Figure 1-2). In this model, learning is viewed as a four-stage cycle: Actual experience is the basis for observation and reflection; observations are then assimilated into a personal theory, from which new implications for action can be deduced; and all of these steps alter how new experiences are perceived and handled (12). According to Kolb and Fry (11), all learners (including faculty who are "learning" to teach) need opportunities to experience each step of the cycle. That is, they need the ability to experience diverse situations (in both the classroom and the clinical setting), to observe and reflect on what they have learned, to develop their own theory and understanding of the world, and to experiment in order for learning to occur. Learning by doing is also an important component of how adults learn (13) because relevance, experience, and applicability are key. In many ways, attention to how you learn—and how you can broaden your experience—can be very helpful.

Learning by Observing
Although the need for adults to learn "by doing" is often discussed in the health professions (14), learning "by observing" is another powerful way in which teachers become better at what they do. This observation might be quite informal (and spontaneous) or more structured (and deliberate). In either case, teachers can learn a great deal from faculty role models.

Interestingly, whereas much has been written about role modeling in clinical teaching of students and residents (15, 16), this powerful method of teaching and learning has not often been described in faculty development. Teachers can actively and consciously seek out role models, observe them, and learn from them. Alternatively, teachers can be influenced by role models through unconscious incorporation of observed behaviors (17). Still another pathway by which teachers can change as a result of observation of role models entails making the unconscious conscious via reflection and abstraction, translating insights into principles and, ultimately, into generalizable strategies and behavioral change. Regardless of the pathway, teachers can learn a great deal by observing or working alongside faculty role models.

Learning From Peer and Student Feedback

Learning from experience can also be heightened by peer feedback and student evaluations. It is unfortunate that teachers are often reluctant to seek feedback from peers. However, it can be very helpful to ask a colleague to observe you and to provide feedback after a specific teaching encounter. This process can sometimes be enhanced if there is an organizational structure to guide a colleague's assessment. As an example, the grid in Table 4-2 can be given to a colleague before a clinical teaching session to guide the feedback process. At other times, sitting down with a colleague and discussing a challenge (or critical incident) and getting a less formal "second opinion" can be equally worthwhile. Soliciting feedback from students and residents can also be beneficial. In fact, a few concise questions can trigger a useful discussion. Sample questions might include the following: What did you learn? What was helpful to you? What could we have done differently to make this encounter more useful to you? It is unfortunate that feedback of this nature is not routine. However, taking the initiative to solicit observations and suggestions can be an integral part of the process of becoming a better teacher. Learner evaluations can also be used with this goal in mind. Teachers may be taken aback by these evaluations, and the opportunity for self-improvement may be missed. Nonetheless, an appreciative inquiry of student or resident evaluations can provide useful information, especially if you ask yourself questions such as: Does a pattern run across diverse evaluations? What am I doing well? What might I do differently? How can I use this as an opportunity for learning about myself and my teaching?

Table 4-2. Checklist for Peer Evaluation of a Teaching Encounter

Teaching Component	Not Done	Done	Done Well
Setting the stage			
Plan ahead			
Orient the student/resident(s)			
Define the goals/objectives			
Conducting the encounter			
Question effectively			
Provide relevant information			
Summarize the issues			
Role model appropriately			
Allow for practice			
Observe the student/resident(s)			
Provide ongoing feedback			
Involve the patient			
Involve the student/resident(s)			
Evaluating and summarizing			
Provide closure			
Evaluate the encounter/session			

Adapted with permission from "Effective Clinical Teaching," a McGill University faculty development workshop.

❖ Becoming a Critically Reflective Teacher

Brookfield (18) has suggested that "critically reflective teaching happens when we identify and scrutinize the assumptions that undergird our work. The most effective way to become aware of these assumptions is to view our practice from different perspectives. Seeing how we think and work through different lenses is the core process of reflective practice." A clinical teacher has framed the role of reflection as follows: "You need to do more than simply teach ... You need to reflect on your teaching, discuss your teaching with other educators, and try to analyze and improve what you are doing" (3).

Schön (19) has articulated the importance of reflection in professional practice. In particular, he has described two kinds of reflective activity: "reflection *in* action," which refers to a spontaneous reaction (thinking on your feet) and "reflection *on* action," which refers to thinking of a situation after it has happened. The former, which is frequently described as a subliminal process of which the participant is only partially aware, is usually triggered by recognition that "something doesn't seem right" (20). This type of reflection also allows the teacher to mentally reconstruct the experience, paying particular attention to context. Reflection *on* action forms a bridge between the re-lived situation and knowledge retrieved from internal memory or other external sources. While the development of the capacity to reflect "in" and "on" action has become an important feature of medical practice, "reflection *for* action" (21) forms an additional avenue for improvement of practice because it involves planning for the next step. As Lachman and Pawlina (21) have observed, "The process of reflection and its basis of critical thinking allows for the integration of theoretical concepts into practice; increased learning through experience; enhanced critical thinking and judgment in complex situations; and the encouragement of student-centred learning."

Given the importance of reflection in professional development, how can teachers promote this course of action? This can vary for different situations and for different individuals. At times, keeping a log of teaching encounters, a diary, or a journal in which challenging situations are described can initiate the process of analysis and reflection; at other times, informal "notes to self" can be very helpful. The questions in Table 4-3 can also be used to guide reflection after a teaching encounter. Some teachers prefer to read these questions and just think about them. Others value the process of carefully answering each question in writing and then reviewing their answers before the next teaching encounter. Viewing oneself on video, with or without a colleague or mentor, can be another valuable trigger for reflection.

How teachers reflect on their teaching practices is a very individual choice. Regardless of the instrument or method, reflection can be very effective as a means to assess and improve one's teaching. Moreover, asking a series of critical questions can help the clinical teacher to break down complex teaching activities into understandable components; to link intent, behavior, and educational outcomes; to facilitate examination of personal assumptions; to encourage "experimentation" and try out new approaches to teaching; to examine the effectiveness of specific teaching practices; and to increase intentionality.

❖ Becoming a Member of a Teaching Community

Palmer (22) has highlighted the notion that teaching and learning require community. So have many clinical teachers, who have noted the benefits of a shared vision, network of committed colleagues, common language, and support for excellence and innovation. As a colleague has said, "If you are able to immerse yourself in a group, it gives you so much. If you start with

Table 4-3. Personal Checklist to Analyze a Teaching Encounter*

Think about your last clinical teaching encounter...

1. What did I do well? What could I have done differently?

2. What did I hope to achieve in this encounter/session (e.g., change in knowledge, attitudes, or skills)? How did I communicate this to the learner?

3. What methods or teaching skills did I use to help the resident/student learn (e.g., questioning, case presentation, one-on-one teaching, role modeling)?

4. How did I allow for appropriate autonomy for the resident/student?

5. How did I provide feedback?

6. Did I have an opportunity to evaluate the resident/student? What was my evaluation based on (e.g., case presentation, observation)?

7. What problems, if any, did I encounter, and how would I address them?

8. What were my "lessons learned" from this experience? What is my "action plan" for my next teaching encounter?

Adapted with permission from Steinert Y. Staff development for clinical teachers. Clin Teach. 2005;2:104-10.

*This worksheet can be used after a single teaching encounter or after a day of teaching in an inpatient or outpatient setting. It can also be helpful to record your thoughts so that you can review them before your next teaching session.

some experience, and you mix yourself into a group with like interests, you get much more out of it .... It's being able to look at things critically with education glasses on ... the same way you would look at a patient with, you know, diagnosis glasses on, or treatment care glasses on. It's a different approach, a different way of looking at things..." (3).

Valuing and Finding Community

Barab and colleagues (23) have defined a community of practice as a "persistent, sustaining, social network of individuals who share and develop an overlapping knowledge base, set of beliefs, values, history and experiences focused on a common practice and/or mutual enterprise." In many ways, becoming a member of a teaching community can be a critical step in becoming a better teacher.

Lave and Wenger (24), whose concept of participatory learning was described in chapter 1, suggest that the success of a community of practice depends on five factors: the existence and sharing by the community of a common goal, the existence and use of knowledge to achieve that goal, the nature and importance of relationships formed among community members, the relationships between the community and those outside it, and the relationship between the work of the community and the value of the activity. A community also requires a shared repertoire of common resources, including language, stories, and practices (25). As a clinical teacher, it is important to *value* the community of which you are a part—celebrating its existence, members, and resources—and to *find* community, building new networks, creating opportunities for exchange and support, and sustaining relationships. The benefit of welcoming new members to this community of teachers can also not be underestimated.

Work-Based Learning

Work-based learning, which is often defined as learning *for* work, learning *at* work, and learning *from* work (26), is closely tied to the notion of community. This concept is fundamental to the development of clinical teachers, for whom "learning on the job" is often the first entry into teaching and education. In fact, it is in the everyday workplace, where teachers conduct their clinical, research, and teaching activities—and where they interact with faculty, colleagues, and students—that learning most often takes place. It is therefore very helpful to view everyday experiences as "learning experiences" and to reflect with colleagues and students on learning that has occurred in the work environment (27). In addition, by working together in a clinical setting and discovering opportunities for learning, teachers can acquire new knowledge and develop novel approaches to problems faced in teaching and learning (24).

Of course, teaching is a social practice, and to be effective, physicians need an environment that supports excellence in teaching and learning. What does this mean? Teachers need to be recognized for their work, they need to feel valued and supported, new ideas and practices need to be welcomed, and teachers need to be encouraged to talk about their teaching. As a junior colleague has commented, "teaching should no longer be kept a secret." The institutions in which teachers work need to create opportunities for effective teaching, feedback, and coaching; encourage diverse models of teaching that enable creativity; and help teachers try to find a balance between the demands of teaching, clinical responsibilities, and scholarly work, while remembering that advocacy for excellence in teaching and learning is a team activity.

Mentorship

A colleague recounts a story in which, during residency, she found a mentor whom she admired and respected. She developed a "taste" for teaching while working with this physician and then decided to pursue teaching as part of her career. And the more she taught (students at first; residents later), the more she enjoyed what she was doing. She also felt that with time, she was able to move from "intuition to intent."

Mentoring, a common strategy to promote the socialization and development of academic medical faculty (28), is a valuable but underused strategy for professional development. Mentors can provide guidance, direction, support, or expertise to clinicians in a variety of settings. They can also help teachers to understand the organizational culture in which they work and introduce them to invaluable professional networks (29). What are the implications of this for teachers who wish to become better? It is important that they identify their needs and actively seek a mentor, knowing that at times multiple mentors for diverse purposes are both recommended and beneficial.

❖ Participating in Faculty Development Programs

What Is Faculty Development?

Faculty development, which refers to that broad range of activities that institutions use to *renew* or *assist* faculty in their multiple roles (30), is fundamental to becoming a better teacher. In many settings, it is a planned program designed to prepare institutions and faculty members for their various roles (31) and to improve an individual's knowledge and skills in the areas of teaching, research, and administration. In diverse ways, the goal of faculty development is to teach faculty members the skills relevant to their institutional and faculty position and to sustain their vitality, both now and in the future (14). For the purpose of this discussion, faculty development will refer to those activities (both formal and informal) that teachers pursue to improve their teaching skills in a variety of settings. The development of clinical teachers as researchers, administrators, or managers will not be addressed.

Faculty development activities are generally designed to improve teacher effectiveness at all levels of the educational continuum (for example, undergraduate, postgraduate, and continuing medical education). Moreover, they are commonly organized by hospitals and medical schools, individual departments or university centers, national or international educational or specialty organizations, and provider organizations (6, 32).

Faculty development designed to improve teaching effectiveness can provide clinicians with new knowledge and skills about teaching and learning. It can also reinforce or alter attitudes or beliefs about education and instruction; provide a conceptual framework for what is often performed intuitively; and introduce clinicians to a community of medical educators interested in enhancing teaching and learning for students, patients, and peers. As a clinical teacher recently commented, "Participating in a faculty development workshop gives me a sense of community, self-awareness, motivation and validation of current practices and beliefs" (3).

What Are Common Faculty Development Goals and Content Areas?

To date, most faculty development programs have focused on teaching improvement. That is, they aim to improve teachers' skills in clinical teaching, small-group facilitation, feedback, and evaluation (33). Many programs also target specific core competencies (such as the teaching and evaluation of communication skills, professionalism, and use of technology in teaching and learning). Less attention has been paid to the personal development of health care professionals, educational leadership and scholarship, and organizational development and change. Clinical teachers should choose their faculty development programs so that their perceived needs and identified goals can be met. Box 4-1 highlights a sample of common faculty development topics designed to promote instructional effectiveness.

Wilkerson and Irby (34) state that comprehensive faculty development programs should include both individual and organizational development. At the *individual* level, faculty development can address *attitudes* and beliefs about teaching and learning; transmit *knowledge* about educational principles and instructional design; and develop *skills* in teaching, curriculum design, and educational leadership. At the *organizational* level, it can help to create opportunities for learning together, empower teachers and reward effective and innovative teaching practices, and address systems issues that can impede effective teaching and learning.

Box 4-1. Common Faculty Development Topics

► Teaching When There Is No Time to Teach
► Actions Speak Louder Than Words: Promoting Interaction in Teaching
► Learning Is Not a Spectator Sport: Effective Small-Group Teaching
► Advanced Clinical Teaching Skills
► Teaching in the Ambulatory Setting
► Teaching Technical and Procedural Skills
► Giving Feedback: Tell It Like It Is?
► Evaluating Students: Truth or Consequences?
► The "Art" of PowerPoint
► The "Problem" Student: Whose Problem Is It?
► Teaching and Evaluating Professionalism

Adapted with permission from Steinert Y. Staff development for clinical teachers. Clin Teach. 2005;2:104-10.

What Are Common Faculty Development Formats?
The most common faculty development formats include workshops, seminars, and short courses; fellowships and advanced degree programs; and longitudinal programs.

Workshops, Seminars, and Short Courses
Workshops are popular because of their inherent flexibility and promotion of active learning. In particular, teachers value a variety of teaching methods within this format, including interactive lectures, small-group discussions and exercises, role plays and simulations, and experiential learning (33). Workshops are commonly used to promote skill acquisition (for example, lecturing or small-group teaching skills), prepare for new curricula (for example, problem-based learning), or help faculty to adapt to new teaching environments (for example, teaching in the ambulatory setting). On the other hand, workshops on leadership skills or curriculum design and innovation can help to prepare teachers for their leadership roles, whereas short courses on research methods and writing for publication can help to prepare clinicians for educational scholarship.

Fellowships and Advanced Degree Programs

Fellowships of varying length, focus, and format, as well as certificate programs, are becoming increasingly popular in many settings (35). In fact, most universities in the United Kingdom now require staff to undertake a university certificate in teaching and learning, and many medical schools are providing fellowship opportunities for advanced educational training (6). Degree programs in medical education are also increasing in popularity (36). These programs can be particularly helpful to individuals interested in acquiring expertise in curricular design, program evaluation, and educational leadership. Although advanced training is not the norm in North America, fellowships and degree programs offer interesting possibilities for scholarship and career advancement.

Longitudinal Programs

Integrated, longitudinal programs have been developed as an alternative to fellowship or degree programs. These initiatives, in which faculty commit 10% to 20% of their time over 1 to 2 years, commonly include university courses, monthly seminars, independent research projects, and involvement in a variety of faculty development activities. Integrated longitudinal programs, such as a teaching scholars program (37), allow teachers to continue to practice and teach while improving their educational knowledge, skills, and scholarship. They also encourage the development of educational leadership and scholarly activity in medical education, and help to create a community of teachers and educators. Many such programs also provide assistance in academic and career development and help to encourage the dissemination of new knowledge to further the field of clinical education.

Peer Coaching

Peer coaching, sometimes called co-teaching, has particular appeal for clinical teachers because it occurs in the practice setting, enables individualized learning, and fosters collaboration (38). Moreover, key elements of peer coaching model aspects of clinical practice (39): the identification of individual learning goals (such as improving specific teaching skills); focused observation of teaching by colleagues; and the provision of feedback, analysis, and support. Peer coaching also allows clinical teachers to learn about each other as they teach together, and in this way, can nurture the professional development of teachers. As stated previously, the observation grid in Table 4-2 can be used as an adjunct to peer coaching.

Self-Directed Learning

Spencer and Jordan (40) have said that self-directed learning is the educational strategy most likely to produce doctors who are prepared for lifelong learning and are capable of meeting the changing needs of patients. Although self-directed and independent learning initiatives have been used extensively in continuing medical education, they are not frequently described in the faculty development literature. However, there is clearly a role for reflection, consultations with colleagues and other health care professionals, self-assessment, and guided readings. In fact, an array of medical education textbooks, journals, Web sites, and organizations are available to inform and support clinical teachers (32). Accessing these resources can further facilitate independent and self-directed learning.

Online Learning
Computer-aided instruction and online learning are closely tied to self-directed learning initiatives. Because time for professional development is limited and the technology to create interactive instructional programs is now in place (41), Web-based learning can offer many possibilities as long as we do not lose sight of the value and importance of working in context, with our colleagues. Online courses also allow for individualized learning targeted to specific needs and the sharing of educational resources.

What Do We Know About the Effectiveness of Faculty?
In 2006, as part of the BEME (Best Evidence in Medical Education) collaboration, an international group of medical educators systematically reviewed the faculty development literature to ascertain the impact of faculty development initiatives on teaching effectiveness in medical education (33). The results of this review indicated that most of the interventions targeted practicing clinicians and included workshops, seminar series, short courses, longitudinal programs, and "other" interventions (such as peer coaching, augmented feedback, and site visits). The study designs of the 53 reviewed articles included six randomized, controlled trials and 47 quasi-experimental studies, of which 31 used a pretest/post-test design. In summary, the BEME review of faculty development initiatives designed to improve teaching effectiveness in medical education reported the following outcomes:
- High satisfaction with faculty development programs
- Changes in attitudes toward teaching and faculty development
- Gains in knowledge and skills
- Changes in teaching behavior.

In other words, participants' overall satisfaction with faculty development programs was high. The participants consistently found programs to be acceptable, useful, and relevant to their objectives. They also valued the methods used, especially those with a practical and skills-based focus. In addition, participants reported positive changes in attitudes toward faculty development *and* teaching as a result of their involvement in these activities. They cited a greater awareness of personal strengths and limitations, increased motivation and enthusiasm for teaching and learning, and a notable appreciation of the benefits of professional development. Participants also reported increased knowledge of educational principles and strategies, as well as gains in teaching skills. Where formal tests of knowledge were used, significant gains were shown. Self-perceived changes in teaching behaviors were consistently reported. While student evaluations did not always reflect participants' perceptions, observed changes in teaching performance were detected by learners.

The BEME review of faculty development initiatives designed to improve teaching effectiveness in medical education also found that the following "key features" contribute to the effectiveness of formal faculty development activities:

- The role of experiential learning—and the importance of applying what had been learned
- The provision of feedback—specifically after new skills are practiced
- Effective peer and colleague relationships—which included the value of peers as role models, the mutual exchange of information and ideas, and the importance of collegial support to promote and retain change
- Well-designed interventions—which followed principles of teaching and learning
- The use of multiple instructional methods to achieve intended objectives—which included a diversity of educational methods within single interventions to accommodate learning styles and preferences.

How Can We Develop an Individualized Plan for Faculty Development?

To participate in faculty development, either formally or informally, represents a significant commitment of time and energy. It is therefore essential that the activity is pertinent to your needs, is relevant and practical, and is educationally sound (38).

The Cycle of Self-Directed Learning

Self-directed learning has been defined as the process by which individuals take the initiative, with or without the help of others, in diagnosing their own learning needs, formulating goals, identifying human and material resources for learning, choosing and implementing appropriate learning strategies, and evaluating learning outcomes (13). Figure 4-2 outlines this process. Following these steps and answering the following questions can

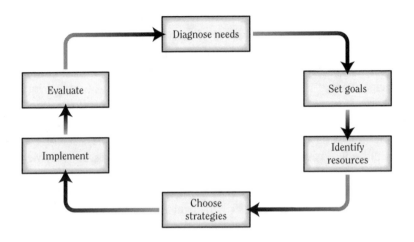

Figure 4-2 The cycle of self-directed learning. From Steinert Y. Staff development for clinical teachers. Clin Teach. 2005;2:104-10. ©2005. Reproduced with permission of John Wiley & Sons Ltd.

be particularly helpful in determining your own faculty development plan: What problem (or need) do you want to address? What stimulated your interest in this problem? What resources will help you to focus on this need? How will new knowledge in this area enhance your practice or expand your expertise?

Determining Your Needs

The continuing medical education literature suggests that learning is more likely to lead to change in practice when needs assessments are conducted, when education is linked to practice, and when personal incentives drive learning (42). Teachers should determine their needs through self-reflection, informed by feedback from students, colleagues, mentors, and educational consultants, and administrators. As previously mentioned, Hesketh and colleagues (6) have described a framework for developing excellence as a clinical educator that includes a series of competencies for teachers. Using this framework (Table 4-1) or others like it (Tables 4-2 and 4-3) can help to identify perceived strengths and weaknesses. As Knowles (13) has said, "adult learners must feel the need for new information in order to learn most effectively"; understanding your own needs is a critical first step, and a wide variety of formal and informal methods can be used (38).

Characteristics of Well-Designed Faculty Development Programs

Features of effective faculty development programs have been described previously. Teachers should know in advance what the *expected learning outcomes* will be, and whether the activity or program will meet their needs. In addition, the program/activity should foster *principles of adult learning* (such as accommodating participants' diverse learning styles, independence, and potential resistance) and acknowledge that adult learning often involves changes in attitudes as well as skills. A *diversity of educational methods and strategies* should also be offered because most adults prefer to learn through experience. It has been said that physicians learn best "by doing," and *experiential learning and reflection* should be promoted whenever possible. *Relevance and practicality* are also key, and for programs to be effective, they must be perceived as relevant to the work setting and to the profession. An *integration of theory with practice* is important, and when possible, learning should be interactive, participatory, and experientially based, using the participants' previous learning and experience as a starting point. The continuing medical education literature has pointed out that much of physicians' clinical learning arises from their practice—and must be integrated with it. The same is true for faculty development.

❖ Pursuing the Joy of Teaching

The process of becoming a better teacher is grounded in the clinician's passion for teaching and a vested interest in the process of self-improvement. Without a fundamental desire (or motivation) to teach—and to improve—it is difficult for any faculty member to invest the time and energy that is needed to enhance knowledge, attitudes, and skills associated with better teaching. Clinical teachers will often say that their sense of reward comes from watching their students and residents mature and develop, and that contributing to the process of "becoming a physician" is what motivates them. Brookfield has said that "we teach to change the world" (18). Whatever the incentive, it is important to pursue your passion and your joy so that you can develop your skills and contribute to the development of the next generation of physicians.

Teaching is a complex and demanding process (8). Becoming a better teacher includes changes in teaching practices, beliefs and attitudes, and, ultimately, student learning. It also includes different processes and multiple strategies, and there is no one formula that suits all teachers. In addition, change takes time, but the result is a rewarding process and a sense of satisfaction with a job well done.

REFERENCES

1. **Brookfield S.** The Skillful Teacher: On Technique, Trust and Responsiveness in the Classroom. San Francisco: Jossey-Bass; 1990.
2. **Hativa N.** Becoming a better teacher: a case of changing the pedagogical knowledge and beliefs of law professors. Instructional Science. 2000;28:491-523.
3. **Steinert Y.** From teacher to medical educator: the spectrum of medical education. Report prepared for the Centre for Medical Education, McGill University; 2008.
4. **Irby DM.** What clinical teachers in medicine need to know. Acad Med. 1994;69:333-42.
5. **Copeland HL, Hewson MG.** Developing and testing an instrument to measure the effectiveness of clinical teaching in an academic medical center. Acad Med. 2000;75:161-6.
6. **Hesketh EA, Bagnall G, Buckley EG, Friedman M, Goodall E, Harden RM, et al.** A framework for developing excellence as a clinical educator. Med Educ. 2001;35:555-64.
7. **Molenaar WM, Zanting A, van Beukelen P, de Grave W, Baane JA, Bustraan JA, et al.** A framework of teaching competencies across the medical education continuum. Med Teach. 2009;31:390-6.
8. **Harden RM, Crosby J.** AMEE Guide No. 20: The good teacher is more than a lecturer—the twelve roles of the teacher. Med Teach. 2000;22:334-47.
9. **McLeod PJ, Steinert Y, Meagher T, McLeod A.** The ABCs of pedagogy for clinical teachers. Med Educ. 2003;37:638-44.
10. **McLeod PJ, Meagher T, Steinert Y, Schuwirth L, McLeod AH.** Clinical teachers' tacit knowledge of basic pedagogic principles. Med Teach. 2004;26:23-7.
11. **Kolb D, Fry R.** Towards an applied theory of experiential learning. In: Cooper C, ed. Theories of Group Processes. London: J Wiley; 1975:33-58.
12. **Boud D, Keogh R, Walker D.** Reflection: Turning Experience Into Learning. London: Kogan Page; 1985.
13. **Knowles MS.** The Modern Practice of Adult Education: From Pedagogy to Androgogy. New York: Cambridge Books; 1988.
14. **Steinert Y.** Developing medical educators: a journey, not a destination. In: Swanwick T, ed. Understanding Medical Education: Evidence, Theory and Practice. Chichester, United Kingdom: Wiley-Blackwell; 2010.
15. **Wright SM, Kern DE, Kolodner K, Howard DM, Brancati FL.** Attributes of excellent attending-physician role models. N Engl J Med. 1998;339:1986-93.
16. **Cruess SR, Cruess RL, Steinert Y.** Role modelling—making the most of a powerful teaching strategy. BMJ. 2008;336:718-21.
17. **Epstein RM, Cole DR, Gawinski BA, Piotrowski-Lee S, Ruddy NB.** How students learn from community-based preceptors. Arch Fam Med. 1998;7:149-54.
18. **Brookfield S.** Becoming a Critically Reflective Teacher. San Francisco: Jossey-Bass; 1995.
19. **Schön D.** The Reflective Practitioner: How Professionals Think in Action. New York: Basic Books; 1983.
20. **Hewson MG.** Reflection in clinical teaching: an analysis of reflection-on-action and its implications for staffing residents. Med Teach. 1991;13:227-31.
21. **Lachman N, Pawlina W.** Integrating professionalism in early medical education: the theory and application of reflective practice in the anatomy curriculum. Clin Anat. 2006;19:456-60.
22. **Palmer PJ.** The Courage to Teach. San Francisco: J Wiley; 1998.
23. **Barab SA, Barnett M, Squire K.** Developing an empirical account of a community of practice: characterizing the essential tensions. Journal of the Learning Sciences. 2002; 11:489-542.

24. **Lave J, Wenger E.** Situated Learning: Legitimate Peripheral Participation. Cambridge, MA: Cambridge Univ Pr; 1991.
25. **Wenger E.** Communities of Practice: Learning, Meaning and Identity. New York: Cambridge Univ Pr; 1999.
26. **Swanwick T.** See one, do one, then what? Faculty development in postgraduate medical education. Postgrad Med J. 2008;84:339-43.
27. **Boud D, Middleton H.** Learning from others at work: communities of practice and informal learning. Journal of Workplace Learning. 2003;15:194-202.
28. **Bligh J.** Mentoring: an invisible support network. Acad Med. 1999;33:2-3.
29. **Walker WO, Kelly PC, Hume RF.** Mentoring for the new millennium. Medical Education Online. 2002;7:15.
30. **Centra J.** Types of faculty development programs. Journal of Higher Education. 1978; 49:151-62.
31. **Bland C, Schmitz C, Stritter F, Henry R, Aluise J.** Successful Faculty in Academic Medicine: Essential Skills and How to Acquire Them. New York: Springer; 1990.
32. **Skeff KM, Stratos GA, Mygdal W, DeWitt TA, Manfred L, Quirk M, et al.** Faculty development. A resource for clinical teachers. J Gen Intern Med. 1997;12 Suppl 2:S56-63.
33. **Steinert Y, Mann K, Centeno A, Dolmans D, Spencer J, Gelula M, et al.** A systematic review of faculty development initiatives designed to improve teaching effectiveness in medical education: BEME Guide No. 8. Med Teach. 2006;28:497-526.
34. **Wilkerson L, Irby DM.** Strategies for improving teaching practices: a comprehensive approach to faculty development. Acad Med. 1998;73:387-96.
35. **Gruppen LD, Simpson D, Searle NS, Robins L, Irby DM, Mullan PB.** Educational fellowship programs: common themes and overarching issues. Acad Med. 2006;81:990-4.
36. **Cohen R, Murnaghan L, Collins J, Pratt D.** An update on master's degrees in medical education. Med Teach. 2005;27:686-92.
37. **Steinert Y, McLeod PJ.** From novice to informed educator: the teaching scholars program for educators in the health sciences. Acad Med. 2006;81:969-74.
38. **Steinert Y.** Staff development for clinical teachers. Clin Teach. 2005;2:104-10.
39. **Flynn SP, Bedinghaus J, Snyder C, Hekelman F.** Peer coaching in clinical teaching: a case report. Fam Med. 1994;26:569-70.
40. **Spencer JA, Jordan RK.** Learner centred approaches in medical education. BMJ. 1999;318:1280-3.
41. **Beasley BW, Kallail KJ, Walling AD, Davis N, Hudson L.** Maximizing the use of a Web-based teaching skills curriculum for community-based volunteer faculty. J Contin Educ Health Prof. 2001;21:158-61.
42. **Grant J.** Learning needs assessment: assessing the need. BMJ. 2002;324:156-9.

5

Keeping Up Your Fund of Knowledge: How Teaching Physicians Can Access Clinical Knowledge, Answer Questions, and Develop Skills for Life-Long Learning

William Hersh, MD, FACP

There was a time, only a few decades ago, when the field of medical informatics was considered obscure. When upon announcing an intention to do a fellowship in this then-nascent field, one would encounter the reaction, "Why would you want to put information on computers when you need to keep it all in your head to be a good doctor?" Of course, few people would say this now in the 21st century, and the research and knowledge required to be an effective physician have increased exponentially. As a result, today's physicians need to be as effective at knowing where to find information as they are at remembering it. Moreover, today's clinical teachers must be able to do that and more. They need to maintain and continuously update their knowledge base, and they need to be able to teach others to do likewise. All clinicians, but especially those who teach, need to master the skills required for accessing knowledge and be critical consumers of the available resources.

In the 1980s, the amount of electronic information was much smaller than it is today, and it was difficult to access because most databases were expensive and accessible only by librarian intermediaries. In the 1990s, a growing amount of electronic information emerged, culminating in the National Library of Medicine's launch of PubMed. Through PubMed, access to MEDLINE and other databases was made free to the world. In the current decade, we have seen fur-

KEY POINTS

- Bibliographic databases provide access to a variety of medical information across different Web sites.
- The most commonly used bibliographic database, which provides not only comprehensive access to the medical literature but also an entry point into it, is MEDLINE, which is most commonly accessed via the PubMed system of the National Library of Medicine.
- Other bibliographic databases provide access to specialized resources, such as clinical practice guidelines and medical education resources.
- Most knowledge-based medical resources, from journals to textbooks to Web sites, are available in full-text form on the Web, although some are available only via subscription.
- A variety of specialized information resources are also available for various purposes, including collections of images, teaching materials, and evidence-based medicine collections.
- Some publishers integrate medical information resources into aggregations that provide linkages within and across those resources.
- Most electronic information resources are easy to search via simple interfaces, but more precise searching can be done by understanding and using more advanced searching interfaces.
- In addition to knowledge of what resources are available and how to search them, today's medical educators must also understand, for themselves as well as their students, that different resources are suited for different information tasks.

ther explosion of online information, such that now almost the entire world's medical literature, as well as secondary aggregated sources of information, is available electronically. Of course, access is still an issue for some, most notably access to journal articles, and especially for those not in academic settings (where libraries typically make these resources freely available through institutional subscriptions).

This chapter begins with a discussion of content, that is, what health and biomedical information resources are available. The goal here is not to present an exhaustive list but rather a representative one that covers the diversity of available content. Next is a discussion of search techniques. The chapter ends with an overview of physician information needs and some practical applications of these systems for medical educators. Some of the material is presented in greater detail in a textbook on this topic (1).

❖ Classification of Health and Biomedical Information

Understanding the access to information is made easier if we have a classification of the different types of information content available electronically (Box 5-1). Admittedly, some of the boundaries between the categories are

---

Box 5-1. Classification of Health and Biomedical Information Content

1. Bibliographic
   a. Literature reference databases
   b. Web catalogs and feeds
   c. Specialized registries

2. Full text
   a. Periodicals
   b. Books and reports
   c. Web collections
   d. Evidence-based medicine resources

3. Annotated
   a. Images
   b. Videos
   c. Citations
   d. Molecular biology and "-omics" fields
   e. Other

4. Aggregations
   a. Consumer
   b. Professional
   c. Body of knowledge
   d. Model organism databases

fuzzy, but this list can be useful to organize thinking of content in these terms.

The first category consists of *bibliographic* content. It includes what was for decades the mainstay of search systems, *literature reference databases*. Also called *bibliographic databases*, this content is still a key online health and biomedical information resource. Even with essentially the entire scientific publishing enterprise online, literature reference databases are still in widespread use as an entry point into the scientific literature (especially because many publishers want to direct people to their resources that require a fee to use). A second, more modern type of bibliographic content includes *Web catalogs and feeds*. There are many Web catalogs, which consist of Web pages that contain mainly links to other Web pages and sites. Web feeds are bibliographic-like streams of information that inform users of new content on Web sites and in other databases. The final type of bibliographic content is the *specialized registry*. This resource is very close to a literature reference database except that it indexes more diverse content than scientific literature.

The second category is *full-text* content. A large component of this content consists of the online versions of periodicals, books, and reports. As already noted, much of this content, from journals to textbooks, is now available electronically. The electronic versions may be enhanced by measures ranging from the provision of supplemental data in a journal article to Web linkages or multimedia content in a textbook. This category also includes specialized textbook-like resources related to evidence-based medicine (EBM). The final component of this category is the Web collection. Admittedly, the diversity of information on Web collections is enormous, and they may include every other type of content described in this chapter. However, in the context of this category, "Web collection" refers to the vast number of static and dynamic Web pages that reside at a discrete Web location.

The third category consists of *annotated* content. I make the subtle distinction between this content and bibliographic content because in the former, the annotation is tightly integrated with the content rather than being in a separate bibliographic database. Annotated content includes images, videos, citation databases, and biomedical research data. The latter are particularly prevalent in molecular biology and the "-omics" fields (such as genomics and proteomics). These types of content are usually annotated with some amount of text and are searched similarly to other types of retrieval systems, although their make-up is predominantly nontextual or text that is nonnarrative.

The final category consists of *aggregations* of the first three categories. Many Web sites consist of collections of different types of content, aggregated to form a coherent resource. This chapter identifies examples of aggregators in biomedical research, clinical content, and consumer content. In one sense, the entire Web can be viewed as one big aggregation, but as we will see, there are plenty of more confined aggregations that provide value within their (not always distinct) boundaries.

❖ Bibliographic Content

Bibliographic content consists of references or citations to complete resources. Bibliographic databases were designed to steer the searcher to printed resources, not to provide the information itself. Most have fields not only for the subject matter, such as the title, abstract, and indexing terms, but also other attributes, such as author name or names, publication date, publication type, and grant identification number. This discussion begins with literature reference databases, followed by descriptions of Web catalogs and feeds and then specialized registries. Although not typically considered bibliographic databases, many Web catalogs and feeds can be viewed as bibliographic in that they provide links to other information sources. Indeed, some modern bibliographic databases offer direct linkage to the literature they are referencing and thus are becoming similar to Web catalogs.

Literature Reference Databases

Produced by the National Center for Biotechnology Information (www.ncbi.nlm.nih.gov) within the National Library of Medicine (NLM, www.nlm.nih.gov), MEDLINE was nearly synonymous with online searching for health care topics for many years. There are actually a substantial number of additional bibliographic databases, which are produced by the NLM and other information providers.

MEDLINE

MEDLINE contains bibliographic references to all the biomedical articles, editorials, letters to the editors, and other content in more than 5000 scientific journals. At present, over 600,000 references are added to MEDLINE each year. Dating back to its inception in 1966, MEDLINE now contains over 16 million references.

MEDLINE has evolved over the years. Additional attributes have been added, such as the secondary source identifier, which provides a link to records in other databases (for example, the GenBank database of gene sequences and the ClinicalTrials.gov database of clinical trials). Other attributes have been enhanced, such as publication type, which lists, for example, whether the article is a meta-analysis, practice guideline, review article, or randomized, controlled trial.

Most users access MEDLINE via the free PubMed system at the NLM (http://pubmed.gov), which provides access to other NLM databases as well. There are other ways to access MEDLINE. Some information vendors, such as Ovid Technologies (www.ovid.com) and Aries Systems (www1.kfinder.com), license the content and provide value-added services that can be accessed for a fee by individuals and institutions.

Other NLM Bibliographic Resources
MEDLINE is only one of many databases produced by the NLM. Not only are many more specialized databases also available, but they are also accessed from a variety of interfaces. While most of these databases are bibliographic, some provide full text. In general, the NLM's other databases have fields defined in ways similar or identical to those used in MEDLINE. The primary interface for journal citations is PubMed, which itself is part of the large Entrez system (www.ncbi.nlm.nih.gov/sites/entrez).

Non-NLM Bibliographic Databases
The NLM is not the sole producer of bibliographic databases. Many other entities, public and private, produce a wide variety of databases. One of these is Scopus (www.scopus.com), a product of Elsevier (www.elsevier.com) that includes 29 million records covering 15,000 journals from 4000 publishers, including 5300 health science journals. Scopus includes links to the full text of articles, as well as cited and citing documents. The database also contains patents and scientific Web pages. Elsevier publishes a subset of these in another database called EMBASE (http://info.embase.com), which is complementary to MEDLINE. EMBASE has a more international focus, including more non–English-language journals. These journals are often important for researchers carrying out systematic reviews and meta-analyses who need access to all the studies done across the world.

Another bibliographic database of sorts, although perhaps an example of how the borders of content classification schema can blur, is Google Scholar (http://scholar.google.com), which contains links to full-text scientific articles on the Web, even those that are protected by passwords (for subscribers).

Other bibliographic databases provide access to online resources. For medical educators, the Association of American Medical Colleges has developed MedEdPORTAL (www.aamc.org/mededportal), a database of peer-

reviewed medical education resources. Each record in the database contains meta-data about the resource, such as its educational objectives and
document type. Also of interest to medical educators and others is HEAL
(Health Education Assets Library; www.healcentral.org), a repository of
free, Web-based multimedia teaching materials in the health sciences.

Web Catalogs and Feeds
Although some may not consider Web catalogs to be bibliographic content,
they share many features with traditional bibliographic databases. A variety
of health-oriented Web catalogs exist, each with unique features. Some are
oriented to health professionals and include the following:

- Intute (www.intute.ac.uk/healthandlifesciences/medicine)—
  formerly called OMNI, a Web catalog maintained by universities in the United Kingdom
- HON Select (www.hon.ch/HONselect)—a European catalog of
  clinician-oriented Web content from the Health on the Net
  Foundation
- Translating Research into Practice (TRIP,
  www.tripdatabase.com)—allows searching over the titles or
  full texts of a wide variety of evidence-based online resources,
  including full-text journals, electronic textbooks, and EBM
  databases

Other Web catalogs are oriented to consumers. Some specific consumer-
oriented catalogs include:

- HealthFinder (www.healthfinder.gov)—consumer-oriented
  health information maintained by the Office of Disease
  Prevention and Health Promotion of the U.S. Department of
  Health and Human Services
- MedStory (www.medstory.com)—recently acquired by
  Microsoft, this site features health information filtered by
  specific "media partners" vetted for producing content of
  high quality
- WebMD (www.webmd.com)—a Web catalog is part of this
  much larger consumer health information site

Specialized Registries
A specialized registry has overlap with literature reference databases and
Web catalogs but can be considered distinct in that it points to more diverse
information resources. One specialized registry of great importance for
health care is the National Guidelines Clearinghouse (www.guideline.gov).
Produced by the Agency for Healthcare Research and Quality (AHRQ), it

contains exhaustive information about clinical practice guidelines. Some of the guidelines produced are freely available, published electronically or on paper. Others are proprietary, in which case a link is provided to a location at which the guideline can be ordered or purchased. The overall goal of the National Guidelines Clearinghouse is to make evidence-based clinical practice guidelines and related abstract, summary, and comparison materials widely available to health care and other professionals.

❖ Full-Text Content

Full-text content contains the complete text of a resource as well as associated tables, figures, images, and other graphics. If a database has a corresponding print version, then the text portions of the electronic and print versions should be nearly identical.

Periodicals

Just about all scientific journals, certainly those in health and biomedicine, are now published electronically. Commercial publishers such as Springer (www.springer.com) and Elsevier (www.elsevier.com) tend to sell vast collections of their journals to large customers, such as libraries, instead of individual subscribers. Many health and biomedical journals published by nonprofit publishers (typically scientific and medical societies) publish their journals electronically though Highwire Press (www.highwire.org). Some well-known journals that use Highwire Press include *Annals of Internal Medicine* (www.annals.org), *British Medical Journal* (www.bmj.com), and *New England Journal of Medicine* (www.nejm.org).

Many government entities provide periodical information in full-text form. Among the best known of these are *Morbidity and Mortality Weekly Report* (www.cdc.gov/mmwr) from the Centers for Disease Control and Prevention and *AHRQ WebM&M: Morbidity & Mortality Rounds on the Web* (www.webmm.ahrq.gov).

Another source for full-text journal articles is the repository PubMed Central (http://pubmedcentral.gov). PubMed Central contains articles from several hundred journals that deposit them. It also includes manuscripts submitted by authors representing research done via funding from National Institutes of Health (NIH) grants, based on an adopted policy that encourages grantees to submit the final document submitted to the journal after peer review but before typesetting.

Books and Reports

An increasing number of textbooks are available in computer form. One of the first textbooks available electronically was *Scientific American Medicine*, now *ACP Medicine* (www.acpmedicine.com). Other venerable print textbooks now available electronically include *Physicians' Desk Reference* (Medical Economics, Inc., www.pdr.net) and the *Merck Manual* (Merck & Co., www.merck.com/mmpe). The latter is one of the few traditional medical textbooks available for free on the Web.

A common approach with textbooks is to bundle them, sometimes with linkages across the aggregated texts. An early bundler of textbooks was *Stat!-Ref* (Teton Data Systems, www.statref.com), which, like many, began as a CD-ROM product and then moved to the Web. *Stat!-Ref* offers more than 30 textbooks. Another early product that implemented linking early was a combination of *Harrison's Principles of Internal Medicine* and the drug reference *U.S. Pharmacopeia*, which are now part of a large collection called *AccessMedicine* (www.accessmedicine.com). Some other well-known providers of multiple online textbooks are MDConsult (www.mdconsult.com) and eMedicine (www.emedicine.com).

Another type of publication long of interest to clinicians in print form is collected summaries of journal articles. Probably the best known among these are the Massachusetts Medical Society's *Journal Watch* (www.jwatch.org) and, from the American College of Physicians (ACP), *ACP Journal Club* (www.acpjc.org). The latter is a supplement to ACP's journal *Annals of Internal Medicine* and uses a highly structured format designed to provide the reader all the important details of the study, including pertinent EBM statistics, such as patient population, intervention, and number needed to treat. Another innovation of *ACP Journal Club* is the STARS system, which provides ratings for "clinical relevance and newsworthiness" from a group of sentinel readers (2).

A growing trend is to redesign full-text information for use on personal digital assistants (PDAs) and smart phones. The advantage of these devices for information retrieval databases is their portability, although they are limited by constraints in screen size and memory capacity. In addition to many of the standard textbooks and references are those designed explicitly for PDAs; probably the best-known is the drug reference ePocrates (www.epocrates.com). Large vendors of PDA-based medical content include Skyscape (www.skyscape.com) and Unbound Medicine (www.unboundmedicine.com).

Web Collections

As noted at the beginning of the chapter, the term "Web collection" is used here for the classification of discrete collections of Web pages providing full-text information. Health-oriented Web sites are produced by everyone from individuals to nonprofit entities to companies to governments. The Web has fundamentally altered the publishing of health information. To begin with, the bar of entry has been significantly lowered. Almost anyone can become a "publisher" of health or any other type of information. The ease of producing and disseminating has had ramifications; for example, the ease of copying content threatens protection of intellectual property, and the ease of posting incorrect or fraudulent information can mislead patients (and even physicians). The Internet, through Web sites, news groups, e-mail lists, and chat rooms, also rapidly speeds the dissemination of information and misinformation. Nonetheless, many Web sites empower the health care provider and consumer alike.

Probably the most effective user of the Web to provide health information is the U.S. government. The bibliographic databases of the NLM, National Cancer Institute, AHRQ, and others have been described. These agencies have also been innovative in providing comprehensive full-text information for health care providers and consumers as well. Some of these (in particular MedlinePlus) are described later in this chapter as aggregations because they provide many different types of resources. Smaller yet still comprehensive Web sites include the following:

- The Diseases and Conditions (www.cdc.gov/DiseasesConditions) and Traveler's Health (www.cdc.gov/travel) Web sites of the Centers for Disease Control and Prevention
- Health information from other NIH institutes besides the NLM, such as the National Cancer Institute (www.cancer.gov), National Institute of Diabetes and Digestive and Kidney Diseases (www.niddk.nih.gov), and the National Heart, Lung, and Blood Institute (www.nhlbi.nih.gov)
- Drug use and regulatory information from the Food and Drug Administration for professionals (http://dailymed.nlm.nih.gov) and consumers (www.fda.gov/consumer)

Several organizations have used the Web to publish the full text of their clinical practice guidelines, including the following:

- American College of Cardiology—www.acc.org/qualityandscience/clinical/statements.htm
- American College of Physicians—www.acponline.org/clinical_information/guidelines

- American Academy of Pediatrics—http://aappolicy. aappublications.org
- Institute for Clinical Systems Improvement— www.icsi.org/guidelines_and_more
- International Diabetes Federation—www.d4pro.com/ diabetesguidelines
- University of California, San Francisco— http://medicine.ucsf.edu/resources/guidelines

Many new types of Web content have achieved prominence in recent years and found use in medicine. One of these is the wiki, or free encyclopedia. Wikis allow any individual in a community to write or edit an entry. This allows massive distributed and collaborative work to be done. For example, the original wiki, Wikipedia (http://en.wikipedia.org/wiki/Main_Page), has millions of entries in a variety of languages, many related to health. Another growing type of Web content is the weblog. More commonly known as a blog, it consists of running commentary on a topic and is usually maintained by a person or community. While probably less widespread for health and biomedical topics, blogs are extremely popular in the political realm. They are also popular in virtual communities with an interest in a diversity of topics.

Evidence-Based Medicine Resources

Although in some ways textbooks and in other ways Web collections, EBM resources deserve special mention because of their unique resources as well as importance to health care. There has been an evolution in EBM to make it more useful for busy clinicians with the emergence of the 4-S model of Haynes (3) (Figure 5-1). This section organizes the description of EBM content into the four levels of that model.

Studies

The ultimate collection of studies themselves, of course, is the full text of the articles describing those studies. Those are among the periodicals described and often accessed via the bibliographic databases discussed earlier. Always popular among clinicians have been summaries of articles, from the abstracts as part of them to more comprehensive overviews, such as those in *ACP Journal Club*.

Syntheses

There has been a growing tendency toward syntheses, usually in the form of systematic reviews, which may include meta-analysis when enough studies exist and are homogeneous enough to have their results combined. Many systematic reviews are published in medical journals, although once that is

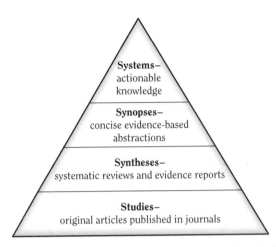

Figure 5-1 Haynes's 4-S model of evidence hierarchy. Reproduced with permission from American College of Physicians.

done, they tend to become static documents that are not updated when new studies become available. This shortcoming has led to the development of the Cochrane Database of Systematic Reviews (www.cochrane.org), which is the largest collection (though far from covering all of medicine) of reviews of health and medical interventions. The Evidence-Based Practice Centers of AHRQ are also a source of systematic reviews (which they call evidence reports).

Synopses
While some EBM purists argue that Up to Date (www.uptodate.com) is not completely evidence-based (for example, statements are not tagged with levels of evidence or support from studies of the highest-quality evidence), the resource is comprehensive and very popular among clinicians as well as those in training. Up to Date has about 4500 topic reviews in adult and pediatric medicine, which are updated continually. Each topic has an outline that allows easy navigation. One of those outline headings is "Recommendations," which quickly gives the specific clinical recommendations for diagnosis or treatment of the problem. Topics are linked to both the MEDLINE references of articles cited and a drug compendium for specific prescribing information. Up to Date also provides a "What's New" area for each clinical topic, describing the latest clinical news in a given field. The system also has links to a drug reference, PubMed MEDLINE references, and patient education information. Another resource in this category is the Physicians' Information and Education Resource (PIER,

http://pier.acponline.org) from ACP. PIER is designed to be the comprehensive information resource for practitioners of adult primary care medicine. PIER is organized into modules that are categorized under seven topic types:

1. Diseases
2. Screening and prevention
3. Complementary/alternative medicine
4. Ethical and legal issues
5. Procedures
6. Quality measures
7. Drug resource

PIER modules also include references, patient information, additional references, and a PDF file of the entire module for printing. A handheld version is also available (http://www.acponline.org/running_practice/technology/mobile_computing/pier_pda), and the underlying system is constructed in a modular way to allow access via other applications, such as electronic health records. PIER has also been licensed, not only by some conventional publishers but also by some electronic health record vendors for context-aware linkage from the medical record.

Every single guidance statement and recommendation in PIER is given a strength of recommendation rating to help the clinician assess the usefulness. The evidence criteria vary for the study type (for example, randomized, controlled trials for therapeutic or preventive interventions). References drawn from the medical literature are also given a level of evidence rating.

Another widely distributed and comprehensive resource is Clinical Evidence (www.clinicalevidence.com). Billed as an "evidence formulary," Clinical Evidence classifies each intervention for a given medical condition into one of several evidence categories. Yet another comprehensive collection of EBM content consists of POEMS ("patient-oriented evidence that matters"), which are short evidence-based synopses. Topics are selected on the basis of whether they address a question faced by physicians, measure outcomes that physicians and their patients care about (such as symptoms, morbidity, quality of life, and mortality), and have the potential to change the way medicine is practiced. The main component of InfoPOEMS (www.infopoems.com) is InfoRetriever, a resource that includes a variety of evidence-based content and tools, including all POEMs, Cochrane Database of Systematic Reviews abstracts, decision support tools, diagnostic calculators supporting selection and interpretation of diagnostic tests and the history and physical examination, summaries of practice guidelines, and the reference *Five-Minute Clinical Consult*.

Systems

According to Haynes's hierarchy, "systems" represent knowledge in information systems that is "actionable," such as alerts or guidelines in an electronic health record. This application is often called *clinical decision support*. The market for systems content is still quite small. Some of the early providers of this content, such as order sets and clinical decision support rules, are Thomson Publishing (http://clinical.thomsonhealthcare.com) and Zynx Health (www.zynx.com).

❖ Annotated Content

As noted earlier, annotated content has its meta-data tightly integrated with the content (as opposed to being in a separate bibliographic database). It includes resources such as images, citation databases, and biomedical research data. Although these types of content are usually annotated with some amount of text, and searched with information retrieval systems, they predominantly consist of nontextual material or nonnarrative text.

Images

Image collections have always been an important part of health care practice, education, and research, and a variety have been made available on the Web. One listing of image sites is available at www.library.uthscsa.edu/internet/ImageDatabases.cfm. Some image collections merit special mention. MyPACS.net (www.mypacs.net) allows clinicians to post and discuss cases. Goldminer (http://goldminer.arrs.org) provides access to images in a group of radiology journals. There are also many commercial image collections available, such as Images.MD (Current Medicine, www.images.md) and VisualDx (Logical Images, www.logicalimages.com/prodVDx.htm). A site of growing prominence for nonmedical images is Flickr (www.flickr.com), which lets individuals upload their pictures and allows anyone to annotate them.

Other Databases

There are a variety of other databases of annotated content. A database specifically worthy of mention is ClinicalTrials.gov. Beginning as a database of clinical trials sponsored by the NIH, ClinicalTrials.gov has taken on a new role with the requirement for registration of clinical trials. After problems were uncovered with postinception protocol changes in clinical trials, the International Committee of Medical Journal Editors adopted a policy of requiring registration at inception of study (4). This policy mandates that clinical trials be registered in ClinicalTrials.gov or other comparable databases before they begin in order to be later published. ClinicalTrials.gov does not contain results of clinical trials, although many advocate that it or other comparable resources provide them. Not only could readers get more details about the results of such trials, but those who carry out systematic reviews would have easier and better access to data.

Aggregations
The real value of the Web, of course, is its ability to aggregate completely disparate information resources. This chapter so far has largely focused on individual resources. This section provides some examples of highly aggregated resources oriented toward consumers and professionals. We will also look in detail at two specific types of aggregations: the body of knowledge and the model organism database.

Consumer Health Aggregations
One of the largest aggregated consumer information resources is MedlinePlus (http://medlineplus.gov) from the NLM. MedlinePlus includes representatives of the types of resources already described, aggregated so they are easily access for a given topic. The selection of MedlinePlus topics is based on analysis of those used by consumers to search for health information on the NLM Web site. Each topic contains links to health information from the NIH and other sources deemed credible by its editorial staff. There are also links to current health news, a medical encyclopedia, drug references, and directories, along with a preformed PubMed search, related to the topic.

Professionals' Content Aggregations
Consumers are not the only group for whom aggregated content has been developed. Some commercial efforts have also attempted to aggregate broad amounts of clinical content along with content about practice management, information technology, and other topics. These include the following:
- MDConsult (www.mdconsult.com)—developed by several leading medical publishers
- Unbound Medicine (www.unboundmedicine.com)—another commercial resource for Web-based and PDA-based clinical content
- Clin-eguide (www.clineguide.com)—combines a summary of diseases and treatments with drug information, full-text resources from the SKOLAR system developed at Stanford, and the database access system Ovid into a single product

- Merck Medicus (www.merckmedicus.com)—developed by the well-known publisher and pharmaceutical house, available to all licensed U.S. physicians, and including such well-known resources as *Harrison's Online*, MDConsult, and Dxplain
- Micromedex Healthcare Series (www.micromedex.com)—integrates many former standalone databases into a comprehensive clinical information resource

The NLM provides many aggregations. One is the Entrez system described earlier in this chapter. Another is the NLM Gateway (http://gateway.nlm.nih.gov), which aims to provide access to all NLM databases within a single searching interface. A more focused but still comprehensive aggregation is ToxNet (http://toxnet.nlm.nih.gov), which includes bibliographic and full-text resources on toxicology and related areas.

Searching

While a detailed discussion of search techniques is beyond the scope of this chapter, it is helpful to provide some general principles for accessing these resources. As with many computer applications, the power of a searching interface is inversely proportional to its complexity. However, modern clinicians, and certainly clinical teachers, should be "power users" when it comes to searching online medical information. Like an expert (and traditional) cardiologist, skilled in auscultation and fully capable of exploiting the diagnostic utility of the stethoscope, the clinician needs to be as expert in exploiting electronic resources. The most powerful yet complex searching interfaces usually are associated with bibliographic databases. However, mastering their use can make searching much more efficient and relevant. While PubMed allows a user to just simply enter terms and retrieve results, the skilled searcher can make much more effective use of it.

Most nonbibliographic search systems provide full-text searching (that is, searching over the words entered by the user). For example, a search on "congestive heart failure" will find articles, Web pages, images, and other material (depending on the search system being used) that contain those words. Most systems do feature more advanced interfaces that allow Boolean (AND, OR) combinations or even word-proximity requirements (such as "congestive heart failure" occurring as a phrase).

Systems also vary in how they display their output. Bibliographic databases typically sort their results by reverse chronologic order. Web search systems such as Google, however, sort their Web page output by a form of popularity, which is how many other Web pages link to them. This approach is highly effective and responsible in part for the quality that most users associate with Google. Non-Web searching interfaces, such as those in electronic textbooks or annotated resources, may sort their output by the frequency of words in the section, image annotation, or other criteria.

❖ Information Needs of Clinical Teachers

Having serially described the various types of online information services and how they are searched, this chapter will bring this together by considering online information resources in the context of information needs of clinical teachers.

Information sources, whether in print or on the computer, are approached for two reasons: the need to locate a particular item of information, such as an article or book, or the need to obtain information on a particular subject. Lancaster and Warner (5) have defined these latter *subject needs* as falling into three categories:

1. The need for help in solving a certain problem or making a decision
2. The need for background information on a topic
3. The need to keep up with information in a given subject area

Lancaster and Warner (5) further note that these needs may also be classified by the amount of information required:

- A single fact
- One or more articles but less than the entire literature on the topic
- A comprehensive search of the literature

The interactions with information systems vary according to these different needs.

Another perspective on information needs comes from EBM. As noted by its proponents, the process of EBM involves three general steps (6):

1. Phrasing a clinical question that is pertinent and answerable
2. Identifying evidence that addresses the question
3. Critically appraising the evidence to determine whether it applies to the patient

The phrasing of the clinical question is often overlooked in the EBM process. There are two general types of clinical question: background questions and foreground questions (7). Background questions ask for general knowledge about a disorder, whereas foreground questions ask for knowledge about managing patients with a disorder. Background questions are generally best answered with textbooks and classic review articles, whereas foreground questions are answered by using EBM techniques. Background questions contain two essential components: a question root with a verb (what, when, how) and a disorder or aspect of a disorder. Examples of background questions include, What causes pneumonia? and When do complications of diabetes usually occur?

Foreground questions have four essential components, based on the PICO mnemonic: the *patient* or *problem*, the *intervention*, the *comparison* intervention (if applicable), and the clinical *outcomes*. Some expand the mnemonic with two additional letters, PICOTS, adding the *time* duration of treatment or follow-up and the *setting* (for example, inpatient or outpatient). There are four major categories of foreground questions:

1. Therapy (or intervention)—benefit of treatment or prevention
2. Diagnosis—test used for diagnosing disease
3. Harm—cause of disease
4. Prognosis—outcome of disease course

As we saw earlier and in Figure 5-1, there is a hierarchy of evidence that provides the evidence in different forms. While busy clinicians at the point of care might seek a synopsis to make a quick clinical decision, they might want to seek a synthesis or even original studies when delving into a topic in more detail. When pursuing a background information need, physicians might seek information in a textbook-like resource, such as a traditional textbook, a resource such as Up to Date, or a classic review article.

❖ Practical Applications for Clinical Teachers: Six Scenarios

1. Suppose that you were an attending physician on a teaching service and knew that the house staff were going to present a case of hemolytic anemia on rounds the next day. Where might you look the night before to refresh your knowledge of that subject?

This is a typical background question, for which you would focus on refreshing and updating your knowledge. You would probably select a comprehensive textbook-like reference. You would access the broad topic of hemolytic anemia and its major aspects by entering it as a search term or navigating through the table of contents to the specific chapter about it.

2. What if a more focused question came up on rounds, such as what is the benefit of diuresis in cor pulmonale? How might you as a teacher access the literature to provide an organized approach to that problem on rounds the next day?

This is more of a foreground question, and you would most likely apply the EBM approach, creating a PICO question. You would determine the characteristics of your specific patient (say an elderly man with cor pulmonale), the intervention (diuresis), the comparison (the different ways you could perform diuresis in this patient), and the desired outcome (improved symptoms, such as increased exercise capacity or reduced mortality).

For this foreground question, you would think of the type of evidence you wanted from the 4-S hierarchy. Because the information need is not acute and you want to present the house staff with more comprehensive information, you would probably seek a synthesis or even original studies (especially if a synthesis had not been performed). A synthesis might be a systematic review published in the journal literature or in the Cochrane Database of Systematic Reviews.

The usual entry point for accessing any type of journal literature is PubMed. For problems like ours, a few different approaches could be used. One would be to enter a search statement (such as *cor pulmonale* AND *diuresis*) and then limit output by publication type (for example, choosing to limit to "randomized controlled trial" or "meta-analysis"). A second option for PubMed would be to use PubMed Clinical Queries, which can be accessed by clicking on "Clinical Queries" in the middle column of the PubMed search window. In this approach, the limits we had to manually select in the first option are done behind the scenes, so we only need to enter the search statement (*cor pulmonale* AND *diuresis*). If you wanted to access a collection of systematic reviews, you might search a resource such as the Cochrane Database of Systematic Reviews or the AHRQ Evidence Reports, which were described earlier in the chapter.

3. Teachers also have more formal academic responsibilities, such as being a course director, or may need to develop a module on, for example, chest radiograph interpretation for residents or students. Where should teachers go first for help with developing a curriculum?

Discussed in greater detail in *Leadership Careers in Medical Education*, another book in the *Teaching Medicine* series (6), developing a curriculum includes assembling information that can be considered more background in nature, so that is where teachers would probably go for subject matter. Curricula already developed by others would be very helpful. These might be found in a variety of sites, such as HEAL or MedEdPORTAL. In addition, figures could also be searched for and used for noncommercial purposes from journals published by Highwire Press, which create PowerPoint slides of figures in their articles.

4. What about the teacher who is asked to prepare a lecture?

In addition to needing subject matter and figures, he or she might need models or other ideas for how the material might be organized. Again, Web search engines or resources such as MedEdPORTAL could provide such content.

5. What about the teacher who appreciates he or she is really out of date on a specific topic, such as use of feeding tubes? How might this deficit be approached?

Although this might be an instance just as well suited for a paper book, most books these days have electronic equivalents that are regularly updated. These updates enable readers to feel more confident that they are getting up-to-date knowledge on a topic.

6. Finally, what can be recommended for teachers who want to be sure they "keep up"? What specific program of regular reading (electronically) might be recommended?

There are also journal article synopses that provide a current awareness of literature recently published, such as *ACP Journal Club* and *Journal Watch*. Another option for current awareness of journal articles is to subscribe to e-mail delivery of their tables of contents for each issue. For example, a general internist might subscribe to the weekly e-mail that comes from *New England Journal of Medicine* or the *Journal of the American Medical Association* or the biweekly e-mail from *Annals of Internal Medicine*.

❖ Conclusion

The search systems described in this chapter and scenarios for their use make clear that finding and applying information is an essential component of 21st-century medicine. Whether it is growing concerns over the quality or cost of care or patients who are increasingly savvy and able to access information themselves, the modern clinician must understand the content and use of online information systems. Teachers have the added responsibilities of orienting their learners to modern information systems, while modeling the behaviors associated with life-long learning.

REFERENCES

1. **Hersh W.** Information Retrieval: A Health and Biomedical Perspective. 3rd ed. New York: Springer; 2009.
2. **Haynes R, Walker-Dilks C.** Having trouble deciding what's most important to read? Look to the stars. ACP Journal Club. 2005;143:A10.
3. **Haynes RB.** Of studies, syntheses, synopses, and systems: the "4S" evolution of services for finding current best evidence [Editorial]. ACP J Club. 2001;134:A11-3.
4. **Deangelis CD, Drazen JM, Frizelle FA, Haug C, Hoey J, Horton R, et al; International Committee of Medical Journal Editors.** Is this clinical trial fully registered? A statement from the International Committee of Medical Journal Editors [Editorial]. JAMA. 2005; 293:2927-9.
5. **Lancaster F, Warner A.** Information Retrieval Today. Arlington, VA: Information Resources Press; 1999.
6. **Straus S, Richardson W, Glasziou B, Haynes RB.** Evidence Based Medicine: How to Practice and Teach EBM. 3rd ed. New York: Churchill Livingstone; 2005.
7. **Sackett D, Straus SE, Richardson., Rosenberg W, Haynes RB.** Evidence-Based Medicine: How to Practice and Teach EBM. New York: Churchill Livingstone; 2000.

Memorable Moments in Teaching and Learning

Memorable Moments in Teaching and Learning

❖ Introduction: The Power of Stories

Even in an era of evidence-based medicine there exists a special place for stories. How else can doctors describe what happened when this particular patient received that treatment, administered by those doctors, on a day when, actually, something very special happened? Should we care about individual incidents? Of course we should. How else will we come to appreciate that for all the rules and guidelines, nothing is more important than how things went with a particular case.

So cases, or stories, have a special place in clinical medicine. What about medical teaching and learning? Should there be a place for stories in a book that discusses the theory and practice of medical education? The editor of this book feels strongly the answer is yes, and the reasons are several. First, evidence suggests that humans think in terms of stories. Just as clinical knowledge tends to be remembered and recalled in a "chunked" format, essentially as compiled cases, so too are memories of teaching encounters—both those that worked and those that did not—recalled as stories, or Memorable Moments, if you will. So if we are to learn from our collective teaching experiences, we need to present the whole story, not just the lesson learned. Second, we tend to understand things better when they are presented in the form of a story. Without the story, we never can appreciate the importance of context or character, nor nuance or tone. Third, stories, like clinical cases, allow us to explore what actually happened. What was so special about a particular teaching encounter? Why did one teaching strategy succeed and another fail? Like cases, stories about teaching tend to be messy. Rarely do they allow for a single interpretation. In that sense, stories capture reality as rules never can; but like rules, stories can be used to solve or at least to recognize problems down the road. Certainly that's true for problems as complex as those encountered by clinical teachers. And finally, stories capture who we are. Anyone who has ever presented or precepted in the clinic, or learned or taught on the wards, is part of the same story: the story of teaching and learning in internal medicine. We identify with certain stories, and understand better who we are and, perhaps, what we are supposed to do.

These Memorable Moments in Teaching and Learning come from the students, residents, and faculty who are all part of the greater medical education story. These vignettes were solicited, then selected, and finally reproduced here in their entirety. All, we believe, are true. Each story is followed by an editor's comment in italics, generally relating what happened in the story to points made in the *Teaching Medicine* series, but also picking up on an aspect of the Memorable Moment from which we all might learn. Like most good stories, these seem to invite as many questions as they do answers. But that's as it should be. Otherwise the stories are not worth telling.

The editors thank all those who contributed Memorable Moments, several of which were recalled from decades past. We hope all the contributors enjoyed reliving their stories, and hope the readers will enjoy them as well.

❖ A Student's First Case Presentation: Joseph Alpert, MD

It was the morning of the second day of my internal medicine third-year clerkship at the Peter Bent Brigham Hospital. The day before, my first day on the rotation, I had been assigned to be on call for the first night. During the night, I worked up a complex cardiology patient who had just been admitted in severe heart failure. He had a loud and continuous murmur across the precordium. What none of us knew at the time was that he had suffered an acute ascending aortic dissection that had extended down into his heart and ruptured into the right atrium. Thus, he had a communication between his aorta and his right atrium producing the continuous murmur. The intern and the senior resident on call with me had also evaluated the patient. The resident told me that the intern would present the case to our attending, the famous pioneer cardiologist Lewis Dexter, the next morning on rounds. Students would not have to present to the attending until we had been on service for 1 week.

The next morning, Dr. Dexter arrived promptly and said to the group, "I heard through the grapevine that you have a very interesting heart patient on the ward. Which student is going to present him to me?" A distinct cold shudder passed down my spine when Dr. Dexter said this because I had been told by the senior resident that I would not be called on to present the patient. The resident explained this to Dr. Dexter. Seeing my pained facial expression, Dr. Dexter came over to me, put his arm around my shoulder, and said, "Come on, present the case to me. I promise that I won't bite." During the next 30 minutes he helped me to present and understand this complex patient in a gentle but extraordinarily skilled fashion. The ward team was astounded when he established the correct diagnosis on the basis of the history and the physical findings alone. His discussion of the differential diagnosis of continuous murmurs resides in my memory to this day, more than 40 years later. That night, when I recounted the happenings of the day to my spouse, I told her, "Now I know what I am going to do for the rest of my career. I want to become a cardiologist and a professor just like Dr. Dexter."

Editor's Comments: *According to the novelist Somerset Maugham, "There are three simple rules for how to write a great novel. Unfortunately, no one knows what they are." What about teaching a medical student who is just beginning his or her third-year clerkship? What are the rules? Do you have students begin as observers, phasing in more responsibility as their skill—and comfort—allow? Do you throw them into the thick of things from the very beginning? After all, isn't that what learning from experience is all about? How do you, as the attending, strike the balance between challenge and support?*

Again, no easy rules here. But how Dr. Dexter handled his nervous novice that first day of his clerkship is instructive. First, Dr. Dexter was clear that he was there for the student. "Which student," he asked, "is going to present [the case] to me?" Second, he listened when the resident explained that the student was not expecting to present the case—in that sense Dr. Dexter appreciated that there were team rules, or at least traditions. But third, he chose not to abide by those rules; encouraging student participation and learning was, for Dr. Dexter, too important. And finally, he was gentle. Not soft, not solicitous, but gentle in the way he encouraged the student with a pleasing quip and a touch, and in the way he "helped [the student] understand and present this complex patient," while still demonstrating his own "extraordinary" skill.

Too bad we don't have a video or even a recording of what actually took place when young Mr. Alpert presented the case to Dr. Dexter. How often did Dr. Dexter interrupt? What sort of questions did he ask? How did he encourage his student to think through the case? We might have learned a great deal. But we do know that attending rounds that morning was about more than aortic dissection and continuous murmurs, particularly for the future Dr. Alpert, who, by the way, did indeed go on to become a cardiologist and a professor—and a leader in his field.

❖ (Not) Alone in the ICU: Suzanne Brandenburg, MD

I remember a night as a second-year medicine resident at our world-renowned pulmonary hospital. In those days, the hospital had an inpatient service with a small intensive care unit; on call nights, the resident was the only physician in house. One night, a patient started to deteriorate quickly. I called the pulmonary fellow and asked him to come in and help me. I had already transferred the patient to the intensive care unit (ICU) and was about to shock him out of an unstable cardiac rhythm. I strongly suspected that I would need to intubate him soon. It was going to be a long and challenging night. My next phone call was a courtesy call to the faculty physician who had been this patient's "lung" doctor for several years. He was not the attending physician on service that month. This faculty member was and is a world-renowned expert on tuberculosis—Dr. M. I updated Dr. M. on his patient's condition and he thanked me for the call. I hung up and quickly went back to work. The pulmonary fellow arrived a few minutes later, and soon after that, Dr. M. walked in to the ICU. He said, "Tell me what to do; let me be your intern. Let me be your medical student." Critical care was not his specialty, but he wanted to help care for his patient. We spent the next several hours stabilizing the patient, and true to his word, Dr. M. assumed the subordinate role. He called down to the lab for critical results, wrote orders, handed the fellow and me materials needed for sterile procedures, and more. Several years later, I mentioned this incident to Dr. M.; while he was very gracious, he did not specifically recall it. What was extraordinary to me at the time was just routine behavior for him.

Can professionalism be taught? As an educator, I'm committed to trying, but I'm not sure if it can. However, as a physician and always a student, I am certain that it can be learned. Dr. M. did not come to the ICU that evening to teach professionalism. He came to care for a patient. I, however, learned much more than how to float a Swan–Ganz catheter.

Editor's Comments: *Why did Dr. M. come in that night, after he was called by the resident in the ICU? Dr. M., after all, was not an intensivist, not even the attending physician on service that month. The pulmonary fellow was already on his way in. We have no reason to believe that Dr. M.*

would bring any special expertise to the critical care situation in the ICU—and he knew it. But still, Dr. M. chose to "come in" in the middle of the night, to do whatever he could to help his patient whom he had been caring for over several years, and to help the resident.

Dr. Brandenburg appropriately asks, Can professionalism be taught? In the Teaching Medicine series, teaching professionalism is discussed most extensively in Mentoring in Academic Medicine *(1), while concepts related to role-modeling are included throughout the series. The essence of professionalism resides in altruism, self-sacrifice, and putting patients first, but also in practicing as part of a system and respecting colleagues. Some authors doubt that professionalism can be taught; they argue that it is not a competency in the sense that reading electrocardiograms is a competency. Professionalism, these authors continue, is a way of behaving, doing what is right, not taking the easier road—particularly when no one is looking. Sort of like role models. What's so interesting about role models is that often times they are unaware they are functioning as such. They just naturally do the right thing. In fact, that adds to the impact role models can have. Learners know when teachers are merely performing versus doing what they otherwise would do (like Dr. M.), even if they are not being observed.*

It is not surprising that even those skeptical educators, who doubt that professionalism can be taught, acknowledge that in special circumstances and settings, it can be learned. So this is the question: If professionalism cannot be taught, at least not as easily as we teach other things, how can it be learned? For Dr. Brandenburg, the question has been answered. Role models are key. Interestingly, her role model that night was playing the role of the intern, actually the medical student: an eminent physician comfortable assuming the role of the student, putting the needs of the patient first. How better to learn what professionalism is all about?

So why did Dr. M. come in that night? One suspects Dr. Brandenburg knows the answer to that question as well.

SUGGESTED READING

Huddle TS. Teaching professionalism: is medical morality a competency? Acad Med. 2005; 80:885-91.

REFERENCE

1. **Humphrey H, ed.** Mentoring in Academic Medicine. Philadelphia: ACP Pr; 2010.

❖ **On the Spot in the VA: Jessica Campbell, MD**

Mr. O. was a patient who captured our empathy. He was getting chemotherapy for acute myeloid leukemia and had been on our service for close to a month. A veteran, he was a stoic man and likable. One morning we noticed that it was his birthday ... and he was neutropenic, febrile, and depressed. We felt sorry for him, and our medical students wanted to do something to lift his spirits. They hatched a plan to present him an ice cream sandwich with a candle on top and sing Happy Birthday." Tears came to his eyes as we sang. He was touched and so were we. We felt honored to be a part of his care. I was proud of my medical students for attending to the emotional needs of their patient.

On the last day of our VA wards month, I was in social work rounds when I was informed that Mr. O. would not be able to leave the hospital any more. Yes, of course, his profound neutropenia would make it potentially lethal for him to be in public places. No, she said, that's not it. Mr. O. had been found in the medical library surfing the Internet for child pornography. You have to be kidding me, I thought, our Mr. O.? It got worse. I learned that he was recently released from jail for molesting a young child. He had been incarcerated numerous times for the same offense. I was shocked and nauseated. My son's face flashed before me at the same time that my unborn daughter kicked me in the ribs.

I left the room completely unsure of how to proceed. Should I tell my team or keep this horrible news to myself? I struggled on the long walk to the conference room where my team was waiting. I was to present a paper on neutropenic fever. I couldn't pretend that I was okay—I was not. As the words came out my mouth, I wished I could swallow them back up again. My team wore expressions of shock and disgust. One of the medical students said, "I can't believe we sang him Happy Birthday'!" Everyone around the table nodded their heads. I understood how they felt. All eyes looked to me. What to say? I cleared my throat. "You know, I'm glad that we did what we did. In our careers we will take care of many people we don't like and many that we do. Our challenge is to treat each of them with the best medicine we have whether we feel they deserve it or not." We went on to discuss how sexual abuse is passed down from generation to generation and that perhaps Mr. O. had been a victim himself.

Mr. O. never did leave the hospital again. His blood counts did not recover, and he developed a severe intraabdominal infection that antibiotics and surgical intervention could not treat.

Editor's Comments: *When it comes down to a teacher's ability to make quick, on-the-spot decisions, no form of teaching can compare with being an inpatient or office attending. "Impromptu" hardly describes the intense deci-*

sion-making required in situations such as the one Dr. Campbell describes. At times like these, for example, when you and your team discover that what you thought you knew about your patient could not be further from the truth; when you are expecting to discuss neutropenic fever, only to find out the patient to whom the entire team was so empathetic is a child molester; when "all eyes looked to me" waiting for the attending to respond—that's when you most need to understand what being a clinical teacher is all about. This is not the time for contemplation. You need to respond at that moment. You need an approach that is practical.

A clever sociologist once commented that there is nothing so practical as a good theory. In chapters 1 and 2 of this book, Bowen and Smith present several learning theories, including social learning theory, which frames the teaching ward as a community in which all members, but particularly the old-timers (that is, the faculty), help to establish the community's values. Teachers, Bowen and Smith explain, "are in positions of power and influence, and for better or for worse, [teachers] become role models for learners." Dr. Campbell appreciated this and more than rose to the challenge. She transformed a difficult moment into a teachable moment. She affirmed her community's values, one including that patients are treated with the best possible medicine, "whether we feel they deserve it or not." Viewed through the lens of social learning theory, Dr. Campbell's on-the-spot decision-making that morning could not have been more on the mark.

❖ Caring for Patients, and Learning From Them: David Fleming, MD

I remember a situation some years ago that still influences how I care for and communicate with my patients. An elderly patient with whom I was very close and for whom I had cared for many years had come to me with weight loss and abdominal pain. As we had feared, a diagnosis of advanced colon cancer was made, from which there was little chance of recovery and for which she ultimately wanted no attempts at curative treatment. We all knew that she would probably die of her cancer soon and that she would probably suffer in the process. When the time came for me to break this news to her and her family, I struggled with my own emotions; as with many of my patients, we had grown close personally as well as professionally over the years. As I faltered to find the courage and words to confirm what she already knew, my patient reached out and gently patted my arm, saying, "It's all right, Doctor; you did what you could, you did it well, and I thank you for that; but it's time to let another Healer take over now." She was at peace with her life and the death that was soon to come; her strength and spiritual wisdom also brought me the peace and courage I was struggling to find. At that moment my patient became the healer and my mentor. That singular moment has stayed with me over the years and has continued to strengthen me as a physician. For the gift of peace I am eternally grateful to the patient who healed me that day.

Editor's Comments: Experiential learning is covered in several chapters in this book, and throughout the Teaching Medicine *series. Why are some experiences learning experiences, changing you profoundly, whereas other experiences just smooth out some rough edges, or deepen the ruts? Many educators believe that for an experience to be a learning experience there needs to be surprise. Something has to look different, catch you off guard, trigger a process of questioning and reflection, leading ultimately to seeing things differently. You go about your business expecting X, but X turns out not to be X but Y. What happens next? Well, it depends. Nothing, if the learner fails to note the difference between X and Y, or if she does not have the time, motivation, or encouragement to consider that things may not be as they seem. But a great deal might happen next if the learner appreciates that Y is so strikingly different from the expected X that she just simply must take note.*

That is what happened in this case when the doctor was so caught off guard as he "struggled with [his] emotions" and "faltered to find the courage and words," only to find comfort from an unexpected source. The stage was set for learning. Now, it could have gone differently. Perhaps if the patient had begun to sob or recoil, Dr. Fleming might have "learned" not to be truthful, or not to strive for fulfillment in his ability to communicate bad news. But that is all part of the humanity of medicine. Sometimes things do not work. But it is so important to take note when they do. The teacher's role in all this is to enable the learner to appreciate just what has transpired, find meaning in each experience, and be able to apply that meaning to similar cases in the future. We do not know whether Dr. Fleming discussed this case with a teacher, but if he had there would have been an opportunity for the teacher to point out how extraordinary our patients often are. And that while the doctor may have the information, often it's the patient who knows. Dr. Fleming now understands that. He learned it from his experience, aided by one of the most important teachers any physician can have.

❖ Tape Record a History? "You Must Be Kidding": William Fogarty, MD

A group of second- and third-year residents were having coffee and discussing cases when a favorite faculty member approached the table and asked whether any of us would like to learn how to take a history. The immediate response was a mixture of laughter and indignation. "We have been doing that since we were third-year students." "You must be kidding."

Kidding he wasn't, and the four of us who agreed to his proposal had the most valuable experience of our residency. We each agreed to tape-record ourselves taking histories and to play them back to the group and the professor. The experience was humiliating, revealing, and, after several tries, ultimately life-changing. We learned that we should let the patient tell the story and that all the minutia we were so anxious to record was much less important than what the patient had to tell us. We also learned, despite great skepticism, that it was also faster and more accurate.

The lessons learned changed my approach to patients and greatly increased the joy of patient care. I learned to listen and to savor the wonderful tales that patients have to tell. Thank you, Dr. Richard Magraw, for changing my life in medicine and for making me a better physician.

Editor's Comments: *Feedback is discussed in chapter 3 of this book, and throughout the entire* Teaching Medicine *series. Strictly defined, feedback is information used to highlight the difference between an actual and an intended outcome. Think of a thermostat relaying information back to a heating or cooling source, indicating that a room is 1 degree too warm, or 2 degrees too cold. That information is feedback. If only feedback in medicine were so simple.*

In medicine we deal not with one-dimensional measures such as the temperature of a room but, rather, with complex activities such as taking a history, which are multidimensional and nuanced. And like ballet, they are best learned in front of a mirror. The teacher's job, then, is to hold up the mirror, to let the learners see.

However, it is not always so straightforward. Not every learner will be perceptive and insightful enough—and secure enough—to see the difference between a well-executed history and one that is clumsy or ineffective. Some may see the difference but have no idea how to change it. Still others may know what changes are needed but lack the motivation to carry them out. Remember, feedback does not energize learners to change; feedback merely points out to learners the direction toward which they need to change, and the distance they need to go.

In Dr. Fogarty's vignette, the feedback worked. Dr. Fogarty and his colleagues were motivated; after all, they volunteered. All they needed was a mirror. Audio- and videotaping work beautifully for this purpose. Then the teacher can sit back, smile, and wait for the sequel.

❖ Not Just Another Weekly CPC: Douglas Forsyth, MD

We all attended Dr. Wordlaw's lectures. Students loved the droll wit of the venerable professor of pathology. His weekly clinicopathologic conference also guaranteed useful information, weighed down with experience. They held out, almost without exception, the promise of either a hilarious repartee or a stunning exposition of a final diagnosis made so simple. The pathologist has the last word because there still abides within the deceased the ultimate cause of death, if only the right questions are asked. But unlike most of his peers in pathology, Donovan Wordlaw had been a physician in the generic sense before he became a pathologist. Some would say that there is a world of difference, unless the pathologist, or any other specialist, was never asked to step outside of his circumscribed role.

On this day, that would be asked of the moderator of the weekly clinicopathologic conference at University Hospital. Dr. Wordlaw, balding and cloaked in his white lab coat, had arisen after the resident, whose late patient was the subject of this conference, had finished formulating his best final cause of death and the guest clinical discussant had committed himself to his own diagnosis. The students and other house staff, tiered in semicircles around the timeworn amphitheater, had handed down their written diagnoses to the chief resident for tabulation. Who got the correct diagnosis and who didn't soon would be known—individually, if not publicly.

Dr. Wordlaw had just begun to discuss each parcel of information related to the case pathology when a side door opened noisily and his secretary hurried in, handed him a note, and hastily withdrew. He adjusted his glasses and stared at the note. He looked up momentarily at vacant faces and then looked down again as if in search of an answer—or strength. Was a storm coming, had someone's wife delivered unexpectedly, had the ailing dean died?

Always able to change questioning faces with an answer and a smile, now Dr. Wordlaw seemed far away. His pause grew more awkward. Finally, he took a deep breath, perhaps it was a sigh, removed his glasses, and with a look of disarming dread he addressed the group. "I deeply regret to inform you that our president has been assassinated.... He has been transferred to the ER at Parkland Memorial in Dallas with a gunshot wound of the head. The vice-president is safe. It appears unlikely that the president will survive."

The amphitheater fell silent as a vacuum, as if it would take time to absorb and organize new information that did not fit into a conference protocol, data that had no place there. But soon silence gave way to gasps of shock, followed only by the sound of squirming in seats. Still, no one spoke. Our thoughts suspended, random images entered our consciousness, like

Dr. Wordlaw's telling us in our admissions interviews that in our medical careers we would see life at its very best ... and at its very worst.

Dr. Wordlaw then offered a prayer for the president's survival and for his family. We had not been aware of his spiritual moorings, and we found it consoling.

After the immediate response to his stunning announcement, still no one spoke. The quiet was ominous. It seemed to say, *wait ... he'll get us through this.*

And he did just that. For the next 20 minutes, Donovan Wordlaw stepped out of his circumscribed role and delivered, with incremental pitch, a spellbinding lecture to this assembly of neophytes on the demands their profession would place on them, as it was placing monumental demands on every physician in that ER in Dallas at that very moment. He left nothing out.

No excuses for not learning the basics. None for not mastering the details. No alibis for not acquiring some new skill or knowledge with each new patient. And no apologies for not learning how to apply knowledge or when judgment enters. We were riveted. We had not seen him in this setting either. It was new to us in a way that so many things would be new to us throughout our careers.

He then continued in a more modulated voice: "But it will not matter to you whether it's the President of the United States or the garbage collector, you had better know what to do and how to do it when *you* are summoned as a physician and *you* are expected to interpose yourself between life and death."

He looked down at his papers, his hands gently, rhythmically shaking. And then, as if having shifted gears, he said, "Now we will continue with today's case since that is what *we* are here to do."

The rest of the hour was spent as if nothing had happened. The final diagnosis was announced on the basis of the autopsy findings. It was not a particularly difficult case, at least not for Dr. Wordlaw.

Still no one spoke. There was no hilarious repartee that day and no stunning exposition. There was much more.

From "The Death Conference," *Atlanta Medicine: the Journal of the Medical Association of Atlanta*

Editor's Comments: *What a privilege it is to teach, and what a responsibility. A medical school class is like an orchestra; the lecture hall a symphony stage. And the teacher? He or she can be the conductor, encouraging learning the way a maestro encourages musicians to perform.*

But, as we all know, life does not always follow the printed program. Many ward teams in teaching hospitals across the nation were on rounds on September 11, 2001. And in New Orleans, several medical services had to contend with the ravages of Hurricane Katrina.

And so teachers need to remember they also are leaders; it's part of the job. One cannot prepare for a moment such as Dr. Wordlaw faced that morning in 1963. But one can prepare to be a leader, as ready as one can be to deal with the unexpected. That is an important theme that emerges from the interviews presented in Leadership Careers in Medical Education *(1), another book in the* Teaching Medicine *series. Dr. Wordlaw left an enormous impression on Dr. Forsyth. The best leaders generally do.*

REFERENCE

1. **Pangaro L, ed.** Leadership Careers in Medical Education. Philadelphia: ACP Pr; 2010.

❖ A Jar in One Hand, A Book in the Other: Seymour (Shimon) Glick, MD

In medical school in the 1950s, before the days of medical student empowerment and entitlement, stress was an almost universal accompaniment of our studies. While most of the stress related to the usual problems of work load and examinations, there was another almost universal worry that concerned us about our future role as physicians. In those days, before the era of Palm Pilots and when a tremendous premium was based on memory, students with the best memories excelled on examinations and were therefore judged by their peers, and also by many of their teachers, as outstanding. I remember that many discussions over coffee related to the question of how to deal with memory failures subsequently in the everyday practice of medicine. We all realized that it was impossible for even the best of us to be infallible and to remember all that was needed in medicine. We worried repeatedly about the problem we might face when, after examining a patient, we would decide on a course of treatment, were ready to write the appropriate prescription, but did not remember the proper dose or manner of use of the drug. The one possibility that was universally ruled out was to look up the information in the presence of the patient. We still lived in the aura of the prestigious stature of the physician who could not possibly show any weakness or fallibility in front of his patient. We believed that having to consult a book or journal would destroy the trust of the patient in the physician. So we spent hours discussing various tricks by means of which we would be able to get the information without showing the patient that we had to look something up. But a single event during one of my electives cured this anxiety.

Among my electives during medical school, I chose to spend a short period with Dr. Isidore Snapper at a small hospital in Brooklyn. Dr. Snapper had been professor of medicine in Amsterdam and had been regarded as perhaps the leading consultant in internal medicine on the European continent before World War II. When the Nazis invaded the Netherlands, Dr. Snapper fled to China, where he was professor of medicine in Peking, and subsequently authored a book, *Chinese Lessons to Western Medicine*. When the war was over, he immigrated to the United States and became Chairman of Medicine at the Mount Sinai Hospital in New York. He thus had the unique experience of having served as professor of medicine on three continents. He was a legend in his own lifetime, and I wanted to spend some time in his presence. During my stay with him, I had the privilege of literally accompanying him in all of his professional activities. One morning a distraught member of his medical staff came in to consult Dr. Snapper holding a jar with an impressive parasitic worm that had emerged from his child's anus. Because of his experience in Asia, Dr. Snapper was appropriately considered the local expert on parasitic diseases. Dr. Snapper immediately identified the parasite as an *Ascaris* and reassured the anxious physician. When asked what to give the child, Dr. Snapper went to his bookshelf: "What are they using now to treat *Ascaris*?"

This was my epiphany! Here was the local expert on the disease, one of the world's most famous physicians, who had no hesitation in demonstrating to his patient that there is no shame in looking up some information in the patient's presence. One may, and should at times, admit ignorance and not fear embarrassment. This was a worthwhile lesson that has kept me in good stead for the next 55 years of my medical career.

Editor's Comments: *This lesson hardly needs explanation. That doctors need not be omniscient is highlighted in chapters 3 and 5 of this book. But before we announce "lesson learned" and go on to the next Memorable Moment, we need to ask why young Dr. Glick was so taken by the sight of Dr. Snapper at his bookshelf, checking on the preferred treatment for ascariasis. Doctors often refer to texts and other sources for information. Why was this so special? The reason is that Dr. Snapper was a giant. Chair of Medicine at Mt. Sinai in New York, a professor of medicine on three continents, Snapper was considered an expert among experts. He even knew about worms!*

In today's world, yes, Snapper would have reached into his pocket and checked Up To Date or PubMed, or any of several of the electronic sources described by Dr. Hersh in chapter 5. But does that mean we all are a click away from being a Snapper? Hardly. Dr. Snapper brought a rich and deep fund of knowledge to his task. When he looked into the jar he knew what he was seeing.

How can such a fund of knowledge be acquired? Hersh points us in the right direction when he appropriately encourages teaching physicians to become proficient in computer systems for information retrieval—that is, know how to find out what you don't know. But that is not to say that physicians can rely on computers to make diagnoses. Remember, Snapper knew what he was looking at. He was an expert. Otherwise, his anxious colleague would not have brought Dr. Snapper the jar in the first place.

❖ On the Private Service: Seymour (Shimon) Glick, MD

It was another busy day in 1960 on the private service at The Mount Sinai Hospital in New York (the administration made it clear to the starting house staff that they had been given the privilege of training at The Mount Sinai Hospital, not to be confused with lesser institutions with similar names). Our attending physicians included some of the best-known names in American medicine. I was a junior resident in medicine rotating on the busy private service, whose attending physicians were among the most sought-after consultants in medicine in New York, and often with egos to match their reputations. I made my rounds on an elderly lady with abdominal pain, fever, and multiple positive blood cultures for a variety of gram-negative bacteria clearly emanating from her digestive tract. Her condition had thus far not responded to the latest antibiotics. After examining her I noted my findings in detail in the chart, together with my suggestions for treatment. I felt that an exploratory laparotomy was indicated. I must admit that I felt a bit pleased with my initiative and eagerly awaited the reaction from her private attending physician. Shortly after my examination the patient was seen by the surgical consultant, the eminent chief of surgery, Dr. John Garlock, who was one of the most dominating individuals in the Mount Sinai medical hierarchy, in an era when empowerment of house staff, patients, or nurses was unheard of. After examining the patient he wrote in the chart, immediately beneath my progress note, "the above note shows that the resident knows nothing about diverticulitis; it should be ignored." I was, of course, devastated, having been so totally demolished by none other than the great chief of surgery.

The patient did not improve and the next day the family did something unheard of at the "great" Mount Sinai Hospital—they called in a consultant from another institution, a prestigious internist, Dr. Dana Atchley, from the Columbia Presbyterian Hospital, to see the patient. After his examination of the patient, a large group of house staff and attending physicians gathered in the conference room eager to hear his conclusions. He recommended

mous role to play in this process as they debrief and ask their students, "So, what did you learn?" "How will you use this case when you encounter similar cases in the future?" Or even, "You seem uncomfortable talking about this patient. That's not a bad thing. How can we make this work to your advantage? Can your discomfort guide your approach to similar situations, not just alcoholics, but to other patients with difficulty controlling habits in the future?" True, sometimes it is best to make a point and say little else. But sometimes the lessons are too important to leave it at that. So many lessons to be learned, so few cases to learn from.

❖ Two Years Later: Richard Kasama, MD

I had joined the faculty at Robert Wood Johnson School of Medicine in Camden, New Jersey, in 2001. My responsibilities included teaching medical students acid-base. For me, this had become a routine. I became seriously ill in 2006 and was unable to return to work until 2008. On the first day I returned to work I made my way to the conference room, where we meet to review and update the status of the hospital service. There, sitting in the room, was a young fourth-year medical student waiting for the meeting to begin. "Hi, Dr. Kasama," he said. "How are you doing?"

I was stunned. I didn't recognize him initially. "How did you remember my name? It's been almost 2 years I've been absent," I said.

"I remembered you from that lecture you gave on acid-base. It was a great lecture that I couldn't forget and made things easier to understand. The other medical students felt the same way," he replied.

At that moment, after having struggled through my illness with many disappointments and discouragement, my spirits were lifted. I thought to myself, this is why I'm in academic medicine, that I might be able to influence young minds and hopefully elevate their love and excitement for medicine. In my Asian cultural background, teachers are revered because of the legacy they leave instilled in their former students.

Editor's Comments: Teaching has been compared to posting a letter. You can be sure when and where you mailed it, but you're never certain that it has been received. Teaching is hard. It also can be frustrating, risky, and even embarrassing. If you haven't experienced at least some of these emotions, then it is clear: You have not been teaching enough. Trust me, you'll feel it.

But that's not to say teaching does not bring special joys, perhaps the most precious that of being recognized by former students, especially when you don't recognize them yourself. There's a delicious feeling of celebrity that comes with being recognized, and then a fulfilling feeling when you learn from your students that they still remember what you taught them, and that it made a difference. Dr. Kasama more than deserved to be reminded why he chose to go into academic medicine and to teach—and so should we all.

❖ Brazen or Bayesian, A Career Is Launched: Jerome Kassirer, MD

In July 1957, during the first week of my internship at the Buffalo General Hospital, I was called early one evening to see a 58-year-old woman who had been admitted with a 2-year history of fatigue, chronic diarrhea, and flashes. She had been in the hospital for nearly 2 weeks. Her diarrhea had worsened 6 months earlier, and by the time of admission she was having three to four stools a day, usually after meals. Her flashes were also brought on by alcohol. She was embarrassed over turning red and sweating in public. I looked over her chart before going to see her and noted that she had lost 14 pounds, she had an enlarged liver, and that on one occasion during her hospitalization she had had four loose stools, flushing of her face and arms, and lower abdominal cramps after ingesting cream in preparation for a gall bladder test. Just before I came to the bedside, the floor nurse said she was shivering, and her blood pressure was 97/70. When I examined her, her lips were blue, but her body and legs looked flushed. I confirmed the liver enlargement. After some minutes, her blood pressure rose spontaneously and the flushing abated. I was convinced that she had the carcinoid syndrome and I said so in the patient's chart.

By the time of my internship I was already subscribing to the *New England Journal of Medicine* and the *American Journal of Medicine*, and in 1956 a case of carcinoid syndrome had been described in the latter (1). I remembered the case because the pathophysiology and biochemistry of the syndrome had been so elegantly worked out. Yet by 1957, only a few cases of carcinoid syndrome had been described; none had ever been seen in Buffalo, and I had never expected to see a case.

Had I known then what I know now about disease prevalence and prior probability, I doubt that I would have been so cocky. In fact, my brashness got me in some trouble because neither the patient's internist nor a consultant gastroenterologist (yes, there were a few in those days) had been able to make a diagnosis, and the patient was already scheduled for an exploratory laparotomy.

I went back to the article, refreshed my memory about tests for carcinoid syndrome, took a sample of the patient's urine to the toxicology laboratory, and asked the technician to run it for 5-hydroxyindoleacetic acid. The lab had never done such a test, but within a day or so reported the result to be greater than four times normal. Had I understood test characteristics then, I might have thought it to be a false-positive, or at least I might have been more reserved in my diagnostic conviction. But I was so convinced that the patient had the carcinoid syndrome that I went back to the chart, wrote that the diagnosis was confirmed by the urine test and, in my youthful brazenness, declared that surgery was not indicated. As you might imagine, many senior clinicians were displeased by my chutzpah. My note was disparaged and ignored, and the surgery went on as scheduled.

At laparotomy the liver, spleen, and omentum were shown to be involved with metastatic lesions, and there was a small firm mass in the stomach. Liver biopsy revealed malignant carcinoid, which was confirmed with argentaffin stains. Little could be done for the patient, and soon thereafter she was discharged.

I now appreciate that my diagnostic reasoning was somewhat imprecise, but as it later transpired, making that diagnosis had a profound effect on my career. I was asked to write up the case for the *Erie County Medical Journal* of the Buffalo Academy of Medicine, and did so (2). The chief of medicine at the Roswell Park Memorial Institute was asked to see the patient because the tumor was so rare. He had heard about my "amazing diagnostic coup," and offered me a 2- month rotation on his oncology service. Years later I learned that my diagnosis of carcinoid syndrome earned me a fellowship in Boston; a letter of recommendation to my program director had conveyed more positives than I probably deserved.

Whether deserved or not, the experience led to a lifelong fascination with diagnostic reasoning. After 10 years of research in acid-base regulation, I spent the next two decades studying diagnosis and the tradeoffs between the risks and benefits of tests and treatments. As editor-in-chief of the *New England Journal of Medicine*, I introduced a pattern recognition installment (Images in Clinical Medicine), an article series designed to elaborate on diagnostic principles (Clinical Problem Solving), and a series of mystery cases that I invited readers to identify. These article types survive to this day.

But by far I derive the greatest satisfaction from interactions with residents at morning report, in which I actively participate on two coasts and in three departments of medicine. After doing so for 40 years, I'm still excited to hear a new set of chief complaints, still in awe of the complexity of the process, still befuddled by difficult cases, and still motivated to explain the pathophysiology once all the facts are in. Diagnosis is a prime function of the internist. We try to get it right with every patient, and from time to time we just get lucky.

Editor's Comments: *In our era of ever-increasing supervision, it is easy to forget that medicine is learned by young doctors driven by their clinical experience with patients, at least some of whom may have carci-*

noid syndrome. Sometimes the learning happens without teachers, or even despite teachers. Clinical teachers are very fortunate; they work with students who are self-motivated, eager to learn, and often downright brilliant. Sometimes the best the teacher can do is to sit back and let it all happen: allow learners to gain their own experience. Experience promotes learning; unforgettable experiences promote learning that is unforgettable. When this happens, it's just nice to be around.

REFERENCES

1. **Sjoerdsma A, Weissbach H, Waldenstrom J.** A clinical, physiologic, and biochemical study of patients with malignant carcinoid (argentaffinoma). Am J Med. 1956;20:520-32.
2. **Kassirer JP.** The malignant carcinoid syndrome: report of a case. Erie County Medical Journal. 1957;August:10-1.

❖ Alphabet Soup for the Soul: Helen Kollus, MD

I had heard that the hospice center rotation was a good one, where I'd learn a lot in a special setting. Indeed, the building was a lovely place on the shore of Lake Erie, where patient rooms bordered a beautiful garden or looked out on the water's edge. It was a welcome change from being on the medicine wards for 12- to 14-hour days.

Making rounds with the attending was a quiet ritual. Here there was silence or quiet music playing that eased the passing of another soul, unlike the din of televisions that was a constant during hospital room visits. Our time was mostly spent adjusting pain medication, treating constipation, and making sure patients felt comfortable. We made certain they suffered as little as possible. Those at the hospice seemed to understand how to help both the patients and their families, who were allowed to visit at any time. I felt privileged to be a part of it.

At my first team meeting with the nurses and a social worker, a paper was distributed that listed patient names, their date of admission, and a column for the patient's diagnosis. As I looked at it I readily recognized the acronyms we use so frequently in medicine. There was a patient with CHF (congestive heart failure), and many others had cancer (LungCA or BreastCA). I have called such abbreviations the "secret code" of medicine when teaching medical students who ask what some series of letters stand for. I tell them they will learn the secret code during residency, but they won't learn the "secret handshake of medicine" until they are attendings!

But I, too, was stumped that day by the "CGB" listed by many patient names on the hospice summary. Is this some acronym for cancer of the gallbladder, I wondered. What else could it be? But there were too many names with the diagnosis. Surely there was no weird epidemic of gallbladder cancer in the hospice!

It wasn't until after the meeting that I asked a nurse about the list. "I was wondering, can you tell me what CGB stands for?"

The nurse laughed a little and said, "It's not really a diagnosis. That's why you don't know it! But, it's the reason many of our patients are here. CGB means 'caregiver breakdown.'"

"Oh, of course," I said. "It must be very difficult for families to care for terminally ill patients who are so sick or dying." CGB is, of course, a condition with which internists are very familiar in the hospital setting. It seems to increase our patient length of stay in the hospital more than almost any other problem. We are always waiting for NH (nursing home) discharges or SNF (skilled-nursing facility) placements when families realize they can't take care of a loved one at home anymore. It was that day I learned that CGB is a problem that sadly affects many other medical settings as well.

Editor's Comments: *As Drs. Bowen and Smith point out in chapters 1 and 2, learning can be conceptualized in several ways, one being through the social learning theory. This theory posits that learning occurs in "communities of practice" where newcomers become old-timers as they move centripetally from the outside to the center, starting with what Lave and Wenger call "legitimate peripheral participation" toward "full participation" and eventually toward mastery. How does this happen? Lave and Wenger describe learning curricula (as opposed to teaching curricula) that consist of situated opportunities in—and here is the key word—communities (1).*

A hospice functions as a community. Could there be a better way to learn the values of compassion and empathy than in a hospice, alongside a community of providers devoted to palliative care? Like all communities, as Dr. Kollus learned, hospices have their own rituals and even their own vernacular and abbreviations. Essential to becoming a part of the community is learning the language, and in so doing adopting the community's values. Bowen and Smith remind us that when a question of learning turns on acquiring or understanding values, then social learning theory is most germane.

Offsite rotations, such as time spent in a hospice, or similar community, can be very powerful learning experiences. One expects that Dr. Kollus will never forget the importance of CGB, even when she is practicing in the NH, SNF, ED, or ICU.

REFERENCE

1. **Lave J, Wenger E.** Situated Learning: Legitimate Peripheral Participation. Cambridge, United Kingdom: Cambridge Univ Pr; 1991.

❖ House Call: Molly Paras, BS

The autumn sky shone brilliantly blue above the cornfields spread out to the horizon, as my preceptor and I drove toward my first house call. This was not to be a usual day in the clinic. The phone call had come urgently, as the health of the young patient had declined rapidly overnight. My preceptor asked me to review the patient's records to provide a better understanding of the situation. I had learned that this long-time patient of my preceptor was only a few years older than me and had already suffered with her disease for years. It had insidiously claimed her life, one piece at a time. She had recently been placed on palliative care with comfort measures after long discussions with her, her family, and my preceptor. I imagined the home I would be walking into and the patient I would be seeing. I pictured a dark atmosphere, the smell of sickness heavy in the air and a withered, lifeless patient at the center. Nothing could have been further from what I was to experience.

When we entered their home, the patient's mother and father were standing in the family room with smiles on their faces. They thanked my preceptor for coming so far to see their daughter, and welcomed me, a complete stranger, with a warm hug. The air smelled not of sickness but of cinnamon. We washed our hands at the bathroom sink and made our way to the patient's bedroom. She was lying under a handmade quilt, with sunlight warming her face. Her body was disfigured from disease and her breaths were shallow, yet she looked peaceful. Her mother lay down beside her and caressed her head; my preceptor kneeled on the floor as we listened to the history. The patient had developed fevers the evening before, was hallucinating throughout the night, and by morning was visibly weakened. As we examined her, she was warm to the touch and her lungs revealed crackles and decreased breath sounds in the left base. She had probably aspirated, as had happened before.

After our physical examination, for the first time since coming into the room, the patient began to speak with whispered conviction. She said she was scared for her mom because she knew her mom would be sad when she was gone. Her mother kissed her forehead and told her not to worry; everything would be all right. I was standing in this room, watching this intimate moment of a mother and daughter gracefully saying their goodbyes. Quiet tears rolled down my face. For the first time in medical school, I was witnessing a patient's dying process, and watching how a strong family copes. I had so many questions. What was the patient feeling? Was she scared? How did she know that the time had come to leave? How did her mom muster so much strength? My questions went unanswered. We sat in that bedroom, not saying a word, just gazing at the tender touch between a mother and her dying daughter.

After saying goodbye to the patient through a long hug, my preceptor took her mother and father into the living room. They asked my preceptor if their daughter was going to be able to recover from this infection. My preceptor, carefully choosing her words, responded that it was likely that this might be the end. Watching the reaction on the parents' faces, I realized that both had known the answer. The patient's mother asked if it was still okay to hope, as it was her duty as a mother to have hope. My preceptor nodded her head. My sight fixated on the pumpkins and bittersweet gathered on the hearth, in celebration of fall. That celebration of the end of life was simple, elegant, and fitting.

As we drove back to the clinic, my preceptor discussed the art of the house call. In this case, it was equally as important to reaffirm and support the family's decision to allow their daughter to pass away quietly as it was to diagnose the source of infection. My preceptor also emphasized the significance of saying goodbye to a patient she had known for so long in order to bring closure for herself.

I wonder how much longer the house call will remain with modern medical practitioners. I was given the opportunity to experience this gift and realize the importance of preventing its extinction. I witnessed so many details of a life that medicine had not been able to save, most of which could never have been gathered in a routine office visit. As I leaned my face against the cool glass of the car window and gazed out into the dazzling blue sky, I watched three ravens soar high on a cross breeze, and I hoped the spirit of the patient, in whatever form she takes, was soaring high above.

Editor's Comments: This poignant recollection comes from a medical student. One suspects she will remember forever the time she spent with her preceptor, making a house call. House calls and similar experiences can illuminate the physician–patient relationship, shinning light on aspects of that relationship that otherwise would remain unseen. Experiences such as house calls are so important for medical students, particularly during their formative years. We can join Ms. Paras in hoping that somehow we can "prevent [the house call's] extinction."

That said, one also needs to recognize what happened after the house call, as Ms. Paras and her preceptor drove through the countryside, back to the clinic. They debriefed. Debriefing, a critical component of experiential learning, is described in chapter 3. Simply put, debriefing is a discussion that follows a learning experience that helps the learner process what has just transpired. It is a form of "reflection upon action" (see chapters 1 and 4) and serves as the capstone for experiential learning. Interestingly, in this particlar experience the preceptor emphasized how important it was that she (the preceptor) reach closure with the dying patient and the patient's family, while also discussing "the art of the house call." All too often this step, the debriefing or reflection upon action, is left out. Here it was included, as the preceptor and student had plenty of time together as they drove back to the clinic. Private time between student and teacher is precious—another reason why house calls are so special.

❖ Lessons Learned "At His Hand": Patricia Peterson, MD

I trained at Parkland Hospital in Dallas, where presenting a case to Dr. Donald Seldin was a cause for fear among those of us who had a less-than-stellar management case. My patient suffered from alcoholism and had come in to the emergency department in the winter with hypothermia, ketoacidosis, and acute alcohol intoxication. My resident and I had taken an approach to managing the several aspects of his mixed metabolic syndrome that was not the same ideal course that Dr. Seldin might have endorsed. After resident rounds, my resident informed me that I was going to present the case at noon rounds (usually the resident would have done so), then disappeared. I was left to bear the brunt of what was sure to be a scolding of some sort. All of my fellow interns, who had heard of the "bad" case, sat in the back of the classroom, waiting for my scourging.

At the end of the presentation, Dr. Seldin made some comments about different thought processes that might have produced a different treatment approach, but in the end, what really mattered was that the patient was recovering and doing well that morning. I was so relieved and had great respect for Dr. Seldin's ability to use the case as a teaching example yet leave my own confidence intact. I learned a lot that day.

Incidentally, my fellow interns were sorely disappointed that they didn't get to witness the expected scenario. I hope that Dr. Seldin would be proud of how I have practiced internal medicine over all these years. I am grateful for the lessons I learned at his hand.

Editor's Comments: *An often expressed concern among modern teaching physicians, including those less senior than the eminent Dr. Seldin, is that we have become "too soft" or "too politically correct." Should we not emulate what (we think) we remember from our own teachers, and set high standards, be uncompromising, and not hold back our critical comments, letting the chips (and medical students) fall where they may?*

Much can be said in favor of this seemingly old-fashioned approach. We know that emotional valence, both joy and fear, heightens memory.

We also should be concerned about trainees' clinical skills if the trainees are reared in an environment in which every answer is correct and nobody is ever wrong. That more contemporary approach may help secure the relationship between teachers and students, but at what cost?

Several observational studies (1) call attention to the extremely light touch used by contemporary clinical teachers when they encounter mistakes. Sometimes, it appears, light touch becomes "no touch." And so mistakes go uncorrected; unprofessional behavior is ignored.

One suspects this never was a problem for Dr. Seldin and his contemporaries, which makes Dr. Peterson's recollection of her encounter with Dr. Seldin so interesting. She remains grateful. Either his bark was worse than his bite or he just knew where and when to criticize, and where and when to praise. Are there guidelines for how "hard" or how "soft" to be? Rules fail here. Delivering criticism is much too complicated for rules. But one thing is certain: Dr. Seldin handled this situation masterfully. To a trembling student he leant support. That word literally means "to hold up," as when you extend your arm to help. And interestingly, Dr. Peterson recalls that she "learned at his hand."

REFERENCE

1. **Pomerantz AM, Ende J, Erickson F.** Precepting conversations in a general medicine clinic. In: Morris GH, Chenail GH, eds. The Talk of the Clinic. Hillsdale, NJ: Lawrence Erlbaum Associates; 1995:151-70.

❖ On Rounds, With the Chief: Peter Rosario, MD

The chief of medicine stood about 6 feet 4 inches tall, making it very difficult to miss his presence in the midwestern teaching hospital where I completed an internship and residency. His stature was equaled by a depth of knowledge fueled by a constant evaluation of the medical and surgical journals, and their respective subspecialty journals, too. Afternoon rounds with the chief were invariably a rich learning experience. Although he was stern toward those who made thoughtless mistakes, his teaching sessions were held with great respect for the students, interns, residents, and patients standing before him. His passion was to share knowledge in hopes of forming excellent doctors and promoting the best in patient care. We would start in the hallway but always seemed to end at the bedside. Most patients felt good to be in the presence of this teacher and his entourage of students, nurses, and doctors. If they were overwhelmed, it was with an awareness of the education being poured forth on their behalf.

One afternoon, an intern presented the history and physical findings of a lady with weight loss and mild anemia. As we stood at the bedside, the chief, true to form, expounded a thorough differential diagnosis that impressed everyone, even the patient. Gastrointestinal disease was in that differential, so he asked whether a rectal examination had been done (this important bit of information had purposefully been eliminated from the presentation—a feeble attempt at one-upmanship by the intern). In fact, one had been done. It indicated a possible rectal mass. This led the chief to ask for an examination glove and to announce to the patient that he would perform a rectal exam. He called on the chief resident to fetch a glove.

The dignity of the human person was never taken lightly by the chief, so we all wondered how this examination was to be done as he placed the glove over his hand. Much to everyone's surprise, the index finger on the glove was missing. As the chief stared, in wonder, at his gloved hand sans the covering for his examining finger, everyone burst out in laughter. Even the patient laughed, and the good nature of the chief of medicine showed through as even he had to chuckle.

The rectal was not completed, and rounds had concluded on a light-hearted note. The patient felt important at having become the center of attention of so many doctors; we felt privileged to have been exposed to a wonderful discussion; and the chief resident, well, he was last seen hurriedly walking down the hall toward the back stairwell with scissors in hand.

Editor's Comments: *The famous novelist and essayist E.B. White once wrote, "Analyzing humor is like dissecting a frog. Few people are interested, and the frog dies of it." So little good will come from our worrying too much about this or that joke on rounds, or whether or not something was funny. But a great deal of good can come from taking note of this chief's rounds, particularly the tone, or what Skeff and others in* Methods for Teaching Medicine *(another book in the* Teaching Medicine *series [1]) refer to as the learning climate.*

Learning climate is a key determinant in the success of any teaching activity, particularly informal ones, such as group discussions or rounds. Is the sun shining? Will learners be encouraged to take risks, ask questions, speak up, ask for help?—all essential to learning regardless of the specific type of teaching that is under way. Or is it cold and gray, and will learners keep their questions and concerns tightly wrapped, like a flowering plant covered to survive the winter?

Recommendations to help establish a favorable learning climate appears throughout this book series and most notably in chapter 1 of Methods for Teaching Medicine. *As Skeff and Stratos comment, the learning climate answers the question, "Do the learners want to be there?"*

Their more formal definition of learning climate is that it represents "the tone or atmosphere of the teaching setting, including whether it is stimulating and whether learners can comfortably identify and address their limitations." Is there a better way for teachers to encourage learners to address their limitations than to chuckle at your own?

REFERENCE

1. **Skeff KM, Stratos GA, eds.** Methods for Teaching Medicine. Philadelphia: ACP Pr; 2010.

❖ Sometimes Better Than You Think: Emran Rouf, MD

As the inpatient month began, one of the fourth-year students caught my attention early on. This was his first inpatient medicine rotation, and it seemed to me that for the first few days he behaved like a kid in a candy store. At 22 years of age and studying medicine right after high school, I suppose I could call him a kid who is aspiring to be a doctor and is excited about learning inpatient medicine. His enthusiasm over diagnosing problems and fixing patient issues often would get him going at the cost of an unorganized case presentation. He is one of the students for whom I serve the role of a docent as part of his combined BA/MD curriculum at the University of Missouri–Kansas City School of Medicine. Let's just call him Sean.

While I understood Sean's biggest shortcoming, I soon realized that I had not sat down with him and other fourth-year students to give them my usual talk about case presentation. So, I set aside time and provided guidelines for Sean and others in a small group setting. Days went by, and I got more absorbed with my usual mix of duties—patient care, paperwork, and managing residents. Sean continued on with the rotation, perhaps with less of my scrutiny, as I shifted my focus to diagnose learning needs with other medical students and trainees. He did seem to improve on his case presentation, although perhaps not to my greatest satisfaction. I had always wanted to give him some real-time feedback but simply was not sure how much I was able to provide during such a busy schedule.

Then came the moment of our brief, mid-month meeting and feedback time. I was hoping that Sean was still staying afloat and keeping his spirits up. I asked him how things were going. He shared his frustrations about case presentation. He also said that he dreaded the morning rounds but that with my help he was improving. I was pleasantly surprised to learn that he had a lot to say about things that I had done and forgotten in the busy pace of inpatient work: "After our mini-lecture on proper case presentation, I felt a lot more confident about how I should be presenting. The first few times

I presented a patient on morning rounds after our lecture, I remember I felt much better. I specifically remember how you pulled me aside and gave me kudos on my improved presentation skills. It was a real confidence booster and made my inpatient experience much better from there on."

As the month went, I continued to think about Sean's remarks, and they served as a booster dose for my teaching!

Editor's Comments: How can clinical teachers take stock and assess their effectiveness? This is always a key step in improving one's effectiveness as a teacher. In chapter 4, Steinert presents a comprehensive approach to gauging one's effectiveness, including reflections, structured formal appraisal, peer coaching, and, of course, student feedback.

Dr. Rouf's recollection highlights that what you think you may be doing—in this case, not providing as much coaching as you would have hoped—may, indeed, not be the case. Sean, the student here, appreciated Dr. Rouf's special attention, the mini-lecture, the well-timed kudos that boosted confidence. For Dr. Rouf this came as a pleasant surprise.

The point here is not whose account is more accurate; the point is, as Steinert notes, when it comes to evaluating your own teaching, no single channel of information will suffice. The good news is that many channels are available. Assessment can be personal and informal, based on reflection and self-appraisal, or it can be structured, incorporating the tools she provides in chapter 4. Video and peer review provide other channels by which teachers can decide, "How am I doing?" As Dr. Rouf found out, sometimes you are doing better than you think.

❖ In the Clinic, Listening: Jennifer S. Smith, MD

In my second year of residency, I was becoming more comfortable with outpatient medicine, by working in our "resident's clinic." I had many excellent teachers. I was puzzled by a new patient to my clinic who had schizophrenia and lived in a group home. She was brought in by her caseworker, who asked that the exam room door be kept open because of the patient's paranoia and anxiety. Her caseworker explained that she was having episodic vomiting. It had been occurring for several weeks. The patient was in her thirties and appeared well nourished. The patient sat in the corner of the room and was mildly guarded in her posture. She had a flat affect but did make eye contact. She was reluctant to have any kind of physical exam, although she did allow me to gently put my stethoscope on her chest. She would not allow an abdominal exam. She would not undress. She was not febrile and was normotensive.

I was at a loss as to how to evaluate her problem. Her caseworker wanted a referral to a specialist, but I could not see how this would help.

As I pondered, I could hear the words of our first teacher: "If you listen to the patient, often the patient will tell you the diagnosis." With nothing to lose, I asked her, "What do you think it is?" Without hesitation the patient replied, "Oh, it's my head. I see people standing in the lobby of our group residence, and I know what they are talking about and my stomach is in knots. I know if I go throw up I will feel better."

I gently suggested to the caseworker and patient that they follow up with her psychiatrist and see if a medication adjustment or therapy could help alleviate the paranoia and anxiousness, and if this failed I would be happy to see her back and proceed from there. This encounter has always been a reminder to me to listen to the patient.

Editor's Comments: *Few admonitions are as important—and work as well—as "always listen to the patient" or, as Dr. Smith's teacher put it, "If you listen to the patient, often the patient will tell you the diagnosis." Such sage advice was part of clinical teaching long before cognitive psychologists turned their attention to how physicians solve problems. But now we understand why, how, and even when these remarkable rules of clinical reasoning work so well.*

As Bowen and Smith explain in chapter 1, physicians use both analytic and nonanalytic reasoning to make diagnoses. The latter is unconscious and rapid; experienced clinicians "just know," probably on the basis of pattern recognition. But sometimes, as with Dr. Smith's patient, physicians don't know; no workable diagnosis seems to fit. It is in such cases —that even experienced physicians consciously summon up rules or heuristics, or ways of fitting symptoms into organized categories of diagnoses. Clinical teachers can enrich their students' repertoire of clinical reasoning skills. Working within the cognitive theory of learning, teachers can provide their students with organizing frameworks (for example, "acute renal failure can be categorized as prerenal, renal, or postrenal") or rules of thumb (for example, "in the elderly, common diagnoses like myocardial infarction can present in uncommon ways"); and then make students aware of the triggers that should suggest they switch from nonanalytic to analytic reasoning. The best rules are brief and memorable. "Listen to the patient" is a perfect example. And as for the triggers that should prompt a learner to invoke more thoughtful analytic reasoning, any version of "when in doubt, think it out" will do.

❖ A Little Night Teaching: Harold Solomon, MD

I was a junior resident at Vanderbilt in 1966, and David Rogers, later dean at Johns Hopkins and the first director of the Robert Wood Johnson Foundation, was chief of medicine. Late one night, he was covering infectious disease consults, and I called him about a patient seizing with pneumococcal sepsis and meningitis. I had never given intrathecal penicillin, so Dr. Rogers came into the hospital, showed us how to care for this patient, and spent the night with us, sharing stories about JFK, staph wound infections, and clinical medicine. His appearance, the eminent chief of medicine, set the standard for me for the subsequent 42 years of my work. He could easily have instructed me by phone, and stayed in bed. What a wonderful example of mentoring!

Editor's Comments: Mentoring, role modeling, counseling, and guiding are discussed throughout this book series, with the most detailed analysis of each function provided in Mentoring in Academic Medicine, *(1), another book in the* Teaching Medicine *series. These functions overlap with each other and with professionalism, with which they share several attributes, including altruism and caring.*

Being an inpatient attending provides many opportunities for the teacher to demonstrate just how much he or she cares, especially at night. Contemporary work hour regulations have not affected the time of day patients become ill, just which resident will be caring for them. To date, teaching attendings are not governed by work hour regulations. And even if they ever were, there are not likely to be rules that restrict teaching attendings from coming in from home.

The message sent when an attending comes in to be with the house staff at night speaks volumes about commitment, caring, and professionalism, but also about teaching. It's one thing to be around when you are supposed to be, and quite another to be around when you are not.

REFERENCE

1. **Humphrey H, ed.** Mentoring in Academic Medicine. Philadelphia: ACP Pr; 2008.

❖ At the Bedside, 39 Years Ago: Michael Weaver, MD

I am a retired general internist and 70 years of age. In March 2008, I was attending the James F. Sullivan, MD, Visiting Professor Dinner at my alma mater, Creighton University School of Medicine in Omaha, Nebraska. The visiting professor for this particular event was Gary Francis, MD (a Creighton Medical School alumnus and cardiovascular investigator at the Cleveland Clinic). In casual conversation before the dinner, Dr. Francis came up to me and told me of a "teaching moment" with me that occurred when he was a first-year house officer and I was chief medicine resident at Creighton University and that he has never forgotten. I had not seen Dr. Francis since that first year of his postgraduate training in 1969–1970. He stated that he was presenting to me the case of a hospitalized patient with mitral insufficiency whom he had been following in the outpatient clinic for a few months who was now an inpatient with congestive heart failure.

He said that after I examined the patient, listening carefully to the patient's heart, I told him that I felt the patient had aortic stenosis rather than mitral insufficiency, pointing out in detail how to distinguish the two murmurs from one another. The patient later underwent further studies and did, in fact, have aortic stenosis. Needless to say, it was a moment of pride for this elderly retired internist that so distinguished a physician as Dr. Francis would relate this recollection to me some 39 years later—sharing this anecdote with me was a significant "teaching moment" for me. I thank Dr. Gary Francis for this moment.

Editor's Comments: If ever there was a single skill that was most likely to resonate with students and residents, that would be bedside physical diagnosis. In chapter 5 of this book, Hersh appropriately calls attention to the importance of clinical teachers' knowledge base and their ability to stay up to date with the latest developments in medical science and therapeutics. Unquestionably, clinical teachers must have strong funds of knowledge. The overlap between fund of knowledge and one's reputation as a teacher is substantial—as it should be. But even today, when patients like the one Dr. Weaver recalls would have had echocardiography long before they were admitted to the hospital, learners cherish the opportunity to improve in physical examination.

How can clinical teachers improve their own physical examination skills? Fortunately, there are many avenues to expertise at the bedside. Texts, DVDs, faculty development courses, simulation, and other modern forms of learning all provide opportunities for faculty, young and old, to sharpen their physical examination skills and to be more comfortable at the bedside. Dr. Weaver recalled a moment spent examining a patient with Dr. Francis almost 40 years ago! Are there any more enduring lessons than those learned at the bedside?

❖ The Author Comes to Class: Steven Weinberger, MD

Over many years as a clinician-educator, I've logged in substantially more teaching hours in clinical settings than in the preclinical environment. Nevertheless, teaching pathophysiology to second-year medical students has always been a particularly gratifying experience—the students are enthusiastic, inquisitive, and thirsty for the knowledge that is increasingly allowing them to enter the hallowed halls of medicine. At the same time, since they are truly novices, they have the ability to make a faculty member feel amazingly knowledgeable, as well as appreciated for his or her contributions to their professional development.

My teaching of preclinical second-year students has been in several settings—in the lecture hall as well as in small-group tutorials. Each setting is rewarding, but each also has its unique challenges. During lectures in large amphitheaters, there is little direct interaction and feedback from students, and it is often difficult to get a sense of whether the students are excited, are bored, or are merely texting their friends about upcoming Friday night social events. In contrast, with tutorials composed of eight students, interactive learning rules the day; there is no hiding of students' interest in, or comprehension of, the material being discussed; and it is pretty hard to be texting friends without being noticed. The faculty member is often challenged to answer those seemingly basic questions that truly test the thoroughness of one's understanding, to simultaneously engage the least involved and the most vocal students, and to diplomatically handle disagreements and the occasional personality conflict between students.

In recent years, I suppose I was somewhat unusual among the group of tutors for the second-year students. Somehow, the tradition over time had become one in which both junior and senior faculty would lecture, but only junior faculty would direct small-group tutorials. As a senior, gray-haired faculty member, I was a rarity among the tutors. I also occupied a somewhat unique position by virtue of having written the textbook that the students were using for the course. So, naturally, they looked up to me as an expert—someone with all the answers to all the questions, all the time. And most of the time, I suppose that was fine, because I was certainly a few steps ahead of them, not by virtue of intelligence or ability, but purely by virtue of age and experience.

One day in tutorial many years ago, we were discussing the case of a patient with AIDS, the initial presentation and some of the infectious complications that the patient had experienced (before the days of highly active antiretroviral therapy). During the patient's course, he developed diffuse pulmonary infiltrates secondary to infection with *Pneumocystis carinii*. Naturally, since this was part of a preclinical pathophysiology course, we focused on much of the basic science underlying the clinical problem. I explained that *Pneumocystis* was an unusual organism that we saw only occasionally in the days before AIDS, pretty much exclusively in the setting of patients who were immunosuppressed by medications affecting cellular immunity. I also mentioned the interesting tidbit that pulmonary infection due to *Pneumocystis* was initially seen decades earlier in malnourished infants, when it was called plasma cell interstitial pneumonia and before the causation by *Pneumocystis* had been recognized. Our tutorial discussion then focused on the nature of the organism and its appearance in tissue. I stressed that although it was somewhat atypical, *Pneumocystis* was a protozoan. Most of the students dutifully copied this relatively useless fact down in their notes. However, one student looked quizzically at me, stating, "I thought *Pneumocystis* was a fungus." Of course, I had to disabuse the student of his incorrect understanding. Not only did I know that it was a protozoan, but I had even written it in my textbook, and as we all know, once it's in black and white in a textbook, it should be considered gospel.

Undaunted, and certainly not afraid of my further attempts to correct him, the student pressed further. "I think I recently read a study in which genetic sequencing showed that *Pneumocystis* was a fungus," he persisted. Uh-oh; maybe time for me to back off a little in my own authoritative view, particularly since I had no idea what study he was talking about. Before changing the subject, I was able to suggest that we both look further into the question, so any contest between student and teacher could be defused.

When researching the subject later in the day, I indeed found an article published a few weeks earlier in *Nature* in which sequencing of ribosomal RNA showed that *Pneumocystis* was more akin to a fungus than a protozoan. At our next tutorial session, I ate my humble pie, while quietly noting to myself my admiration for a student who was reading *Nature* on the side and was willing to stand up to me to correct my error. Charles Sidney Burwell, former dean of Harvard Medical School from 1935 to 1949, stressed to the medical students that half of what they were learning was incorrect; what troubled him was that he didn't know which half (1). That point was clearly driven home to me by this memorable moment of my teaching. Though we all hope that the 50% figure is an exaggeration, we still must admit the truth that "teaching is the fine art of imparting knowledge without possessing it" (2).

Editor's Comments: *Teaching is about taking risks, sometimes even when you don't know you are taking them. Clinical teachers, including Dr. Weinberger, know that all too well. A patient is presented—an unknown, if you will—and almost certainly there will be aspects of the pathophysiology, diagnosis, or therapeutics that will be difficult to discern. So we all proceed with some degree of caution, our recommendations coupled with "could be" or "might be" lest we profess something as true, only to discover* *later that we, the professors, were wrong. Err too far on the side of caution and you risk being seen as wishy-washy. Sometimes you just can't win.*

Dr. Weinberger's vignette makes us even more aware of the risks we take as clinical teachers, even when we possess expertise. True, our job as teachers is not to substantiate our expertise; CVs do that. Our job should be to encourage learning. Perhaps an occasional "mistake" works well in that regard. Keep the students awake. Give them a chance to shine—nothing wrong with that. But still, it's more fun to be right than wrong. So congratulate Dr. Weinberger and thank him for sharing his piece of humble pie. We all are human. Not much risk in that conclusion, is there?

REFERENCES

1. **Weber B.** Daniel C. Tosteson, longtime dean who reshaped Harvard Medical School, dies at 84. New York Times. Accessed at www.nytimes.com/2009/06/03/education/03tosteson.html
2. **Metcalf F, ed.** *The Penguin Dictionary of Jokes, Wisecracks, Quips and Quotes.* London: Viking; 1993:209.

❖ On Rounds, in a Circle: David West, MD

I was a third-year medical student at the State University of New York, Downstate Medical Center in Brooklyn, New York, from July 1979 to June 1980. I recall rotating through my third-year internal medicine clerkship at our main teaching hospital, Kings County Hospital. Our rotation was on a very vigorous, extremely busy medical service. The service included about five medical students who acted like interns, three interns, one second- or third-year resident, a rotating chief resident, and the attending. Most of our cases were very complex, usually involving several comorbid conditions in a city hospital. Our attending was an older gentleman by the name of Martin Metz. Dr. Metz was a general internist of the "old school" who had tremendous passion for high-quality medical care and tremendous compassion for patients. He wore glasses, was moderately overweight, and often wore a bow tie.

Many of our patients over the 3-month rotation required surgical procedures of one kind or another, most of them complicated. I recall one particular surgical referral from our service that was expected to be relatively uncomplicated. I cannot recall the specific procedure, but I do remember it was considered "minor." The procedure did not go as we hoped, and the patient had a surprisingly complicated postoperative course.

Dr. Metz was most disappointed, as one might expect, because this patient was on his service. During rounds one morning, as we were rounding on this patient, Dr. Metz gathered all of us (about 10 of us total) in a circle with him in the middle and made the following comment: "There are minor surgeons out there, but no surgery is minor!" There was total silence among all of us as we looked at him in the middle of the circle. He then made a 360° turn and briefly stared at each one of us to make certain we all heard and paid attention to what he said. I have never forgotten that moment, now almost 30 years ago. I always recall that comment whenever I refer one of my patients for surgical consultation!

Editor's Comments: A book by Manning and DeBakey, appropriately titled Medicine: Preserving the Passion, *includes an anecdote attributed to the famous hematologist and eminent teacher Richard Vilter. The story goes that one of Dr. Vilter's former residents mustered his courage one day and asked Dr. Vilter, "You are such a marvelous clinician. To what do you attribute your success?" Vilter replied, "Good judgment." The questioner thought for a moment and, not completely satisfied with the response, asked, "But Dr. Vilter, to what do you attribute your good judgment?" Vilter replied, "Experience." Still not satisfied, the questioner pursued it one step further. "But Dr. Vilter, how does one gain experience?" Vilter's response, "Bad judgment."*

Medical services should be designed to prevent mistakes, not celebrate them. But mistakes do happen. And when they do, they either can be brushed aside, discussed discreetly and indirectly. Or they can be featured and framed in a way that enables everyone not only to learn from the mistake but never to forget it.

Dr. West shares a memory from 30 years ago that he has never forgotten. Would that all our "lessons" live in the minds of our students for so long. Why is this memory so indelible? Because mistakes are difficult to forget? Yes. But this particular mistake—an adverse outcome in a patient sent to surgery—occurred decades ago, in the context of an "extremely busy" and high-acuity inner-city hospital, one of "numerous patients over the month [who] required surgical procedures of one kind or another." Because there was an element of surprise, as this particular patient fared poorly after a procedure that had been considered "minor"? Also true. But there is another explanation for why this memory endures.

Note how Dr. Metz shared the lesson with his team. Imagine the scene: a somewhat rotund Dr. Metz, probably wearing his characteristic bowtie, gathered the team of 10 around him, and provides a memorable, terse statement; not a paragraph but a darn good one-liner, complete with a play on words. Not a long explanation, just a well-chosen sentence by a teacher who obviously knew how to choose his words. And then, further, he rotates around and stares (briefly) at each member of the team. Thirty years ago and Dr. West probably still can hear the silence.

In several chapters of the Teaching Medicine *series, particularly in* Teaching in the Hospital *(1), authors discuss teaching as a performance, including the importance of how the group is arranged, whether you should sit or stand, how to use one's physical presence, turning, pausing, and so forth—the choreographic and, indeed, theatrical, aspects of good teaching, basically using channels other than just words to broadcast your message. Of course, Dr. Metz was not acting. He was speaking from the heart. He was an "old school" internist who did not shy away from showing his passion. We all can learn from this.*

REFERENCE

1. **Wiese J, ed.** Teaching in the Hospital. Philadelphia: ACP Pr; 2010.

❖ A Snowy Day: Anonymous

A thick blanket of snow covered our city and medical school campus early one morning in January, silencing the air that was usually filled with bustling activity. All of the students received word that the campus was officially closed, and we were to contact our attending to see if we should make our way into the hospitals. I was scheduled to attend the VA clinic that day with another student and our internal medicine clerkship director; however, given the inclement weather he had contacted us and provided the option of not risking the commute and instead spending the day at home studying. I definitely could have used the hours with my books, I thought, given that our national shelf exam was a few days away; but a part of me also felt guilty about abandoning the few patients who may have trekked in for their scheduled visits. And so, I also dug my car out of the snow banks and made a path over to clinic.

Our usual format for the day was to see a few patients on our own as students, discuss them with our attending, write the notes, and go over a small case presentation to pinpoint some key learning points. But this day, I found myself in the clinic with my attending and one lone patient who had driven over 2 hours to make his appointment. Unlike some busier days, I had more than ample time to take a focused history and do a physical exam on this dedicated patient. After I was finished, I sat with my attending and presented my findings. We then re-entered the room and proceeded to talk to the patient together. As my attending spoke to this gentleman, he stood at my side and reiterated the information I had collected, speaking of me as his "young colleague," not simply the "medical student." He spent over 30 minutes in the exam room with this patient and me, quietly demonstrating physical examination techniques and subtleties that I had overlooked. At the end of the visit, the patient thanked us both for our time and left the empty clinic.

It would have been easy to finish the day early, and I'm sure my attending had a multitude of things he would have been able to get done on this unanticipated "snow day," instead of hanging out at the VA with a token medical student. Instead, he asked me if I wanted to stay for awhile longer and go over one of his favorite cases with him—a case that he had when he was in his internal medicine fellowship years ago. I gratefully accepted this proposal; not only did I appreciate that I needed all the clinical exposure I could get, but I also had not had the opportunity to spend much time with him during this medicine clerkship. For the next hour or two, we worked through a case of a patient with hyperkalemia, meandering from the realm of electrocardiograms to cellular pathogenesis to fluid/electrolyte balance and back again. Throughout this process, he talked me through the relevant literature and schematics related to our discussions, while patiently probing me with questions to help me think through the physiology. At the end of the day, I had learned more in those few hours with him than I could have learned in a week with my review books. I have never forgotten that case, and every time I see a high potassium level on a basic metabolic panel, I am reminded of it. More profoundly, however, is what that day taught me about being a teacher. This selfless and generous giving of his time and the manner in which he treated me truly as a "young colleague" completely opened my heart and mind to learning in a way I had never before experienced. It made being taught by him a gift, one that I could not bear to waste. I can only hope that one day I will be able to pass this act of kindness and selflessness on to students of my own so that they may become both better learners and teachers, as I believe this experience has made me.

Editor's Comments: *Kenneth M. Ludmerer, MD, followed his Pulitzer Prize–winning book,* Learning to Heal *(1) with an equally important contribution to the history of medical education,* Time to Heal *(2). In the second book, commenting on a specific program in which funding was set aside to allow ample contact between faculty and students in an outpatient office, Ludmerer wrote, "Learners benefited from having sufficient time to evaluate patients thoroughly and discuss cases with instructors. This was in marked contrast to most outpatient clinics, where the hustle and bustle led to poor supervision, little teaching, and the exposure of students to slipshod methods." "Time," Ludmerer concludes, "was the irreducible element of good medical education, whatever clinical setting happen to be used."*

Pray for snow.

REFERENCES

1. **Ludmerer KM.** Learning to Heal: The Development of American Medical Education. Baltimore: Johns Hopkins Univ Pr; 1996
2. **Ludmerer KM.** Time to Heal: American Medical Education from the Turn of the Century to the Era of Managed Care. New York: Oxford Univ Pr; 1999.

Index